Praise for *Think Two Products Ahead*

"Creating loyalty beyond reason and moving from irreplaceable to irresistible is job #1 for all marketers today. Ben's book will help you get there."

— **Kevin Roberts**, CEO, Saatchi & Saatchi Worldwide

"Ben will teach you how to turn every first sale into residual streams of income with products and services that literally compel a second, third, and fourth purchase. If you have a Millionaire Mind you've just chosen to buy this book."

— **T. Harv Eker**, Author of the *New York Times* #1 Best Seller *Secrets of the Millionaire Mind*

"Wow! It's good. I could write 156 pages of praise for your insight and writing ability, but I have to tackle updating 356 pages of *Guerrilla Marketing* so I kept it terse."

— **Jay Conrad Levinson**, Author of *Guerrilla Marketing*

"I call Ben whenever I have a question about branding and he makes everything clear and even easy and obvious. *Think Two Products Ahead* is like talking with Ben because every chapter gives you newfound clarity and you see how easy and profitable branding really should be."

— **David Doyle**, Vice President, Program Development, Animal Planet

"For a guy like me who used to absolutely, positively hate branding, this book is a revelation. Finally, a clear-cut confessional from someone who has actually worked in the deep carpets with the guys and guyettes in the designer suits. But Ben generously goes beyond the Wizard of Oz exposé (that takes down the scam Madison Avenue and its provincial cousins have been running on businesses for years) and tells you what's good about branding, and how you can cash in on it for your business. I mean exactly, step-by-step. If you are in business and you have anything to do with marketing, you need this book."

—**David Garfinkel**, Author of
*Advertising Headlines That Make
You Rich*

Praise for Ben Mack's previous book *Poker Without Cards*

"As a result of this book, Ben will never work in advertising again."

—**Douglas Rushkoff**, Author of
Coercion and *Media Virus!*

"*Poker Without Cards* reveals the hard-to-swallow truth that one cannot know reality until one understands memetics and poker. Is the world ready for such a revelation?"

—**Richard Brodie**, Author of *Virus
of the Mind: The New Science of the
Meme*; Computer programmer
who wrote the original MS Word

THINK TWO PRODUCTS AHEAD

Secrets the Big Advertising Agencies
Don't Want You to Know and
How to Use Them for Bigger Profits

BEN MACK

John Wiley & Sons, Inc.

Published by John Wiley & Sons, Inc., Hoboken, New Jersey.
Published simultaneously in Canada.

For general information on our other products and services or for technical support, please contact our Customer Care Department within the United States at (800) 762-2974, outside the United States at (317) 572-3993 or fax (317) 572-4002.

Wiley also publishes its books in a variety of electronic formats. Some content that appears in print may not be available in electronic books. For more information about Wiley products, visit our web site at www.wiley.com.

Library of Congress Cataloging-in-Publication Data:

Mack, Ben, 1968–
    Think two products ahead: secrets the big advertising agencies don't want you to know and how to use them for bigger profits / Ben Mack.
        p.   cm.
Includes index.
ISBN-13: 978-0-470-05576-2 (cloth)
ISBN-10: 0-470-05576-6 (cloth)
    1. Product management.   2. Marketing.   3. Brand management.
4. Entrepreneurship.   I. Title.
HF5415.15.M265   2007
658.5'03—dc22

                                                                2006016568

Printed in the United States of America.

10   9   8   7   6   5   4   3   2   1

Contents

Foreword

Branding is simultaneously everything that is wrong with two distinctly different marketing worlds: the Direct Marketing (DM) world and Madison Avenue.

Direct Marketing cares very little for branding. The inhabitants of this world are almost purely focused on "right now money" and as such do very little to build long-term "brand equity" in anything they do. Yes, sometimes Direct Marketers build a healthy second-glass profit stream (the ones that last do), but in general, once the direct marketing stops, so do the profits.

Madison Avenue at times focuses almost exclusively on branding, forsaking "right now profits" completely. In fact, branding becomes an excuse for failed marketing campaigns.

Advertiser: "Hey, this campaign had a negative return on investment."

Account Rep: "Don't worry—there was a branding effect."

It's exactly that conversation with the less scrupulous advertising account reps that has caused Direct Marketers to spout the word branding like a swear word: "Branding!?" And that fairly well sums up the main difference between these two worlds of marketing.

But the DMers and the Madison Avenue guys are more similar than they'd like to admit. Both worlds are guilty of doing something Ben is about to teach you to do: Use the power of sin and emotion to create an irrational connection with a product in the mind of the buyer.

They will tell you, "People are irrational, so you must take advantage of that in order to make the sale."

I think that's hogwash.

If all of the factors were lined up just right, just about anyone could probably kill as well—or so the psychologists say. Should we therefore appeal to "the murderer in everyone" in our marketing?

"Hey, in the right circumstances, everyone could commit murder. So I suggest this headline for your campaign: Use Our Perfume and Murder Those Other Nappy Ass Bitches Who Want Your Man."

Yes, people can in fact be irrational. Heck, we're probably *mostly* irrational beings. But that fact doesn't mean you can't sell by being rational and honest.

This roller-coaster ride of a book totally deconstructs branding so anyone can understand it. It's not rocket science, and it took someone of Ben's intellect to prove that. Ben also shows you how to combine Madison Avenue level branding with Direct Marketing sensibility to create a formidable profit machine.

Shhh! That's a secret many of us in the know have been jealously guarding for years.

Another secret is that if you actually complete this book (there is a 70 percent chance that you won't, not because it sucks—it doesn't— but because most people are lazy), there is an even smaller chance that you'll actually do anything with the information herein.

My only beef with this book is that he panders to what I feel to be antiquated notions that people are weak and evil. Well, I guess we *can* be weak and evil. We can also be strong, good, fair, noble, and honest. I choose to focus on that side of humanity and market to them as such.

You *can* market to the better side of humanity and still reap amazing profits. In fact, history has proven that ultimately you will be *more* profitable if you do.

Overlooking Ben's bleak view of humanity, I wholeheartedly endorse this book.

If you are already prejudging Ben as some master of evil, you should temper that with the knowledge that Ben is merely deconstructing the methods that are already in use by the marketing power elite. These ideas, while supportive of a nihilistic world view, are widely accepted and practiced throughout much of the marketing world.

Now, it should be noted that Ben is a very close friend of mine. If he weren't, he probably would have never allowed an infidel like me to step in here and tell you that he's wrong. See, it's not that I'm wrong or Ben's right. We just have very different views of the world, and we both understand that.

What's important is that Ben's ideas work. Whether you're interested in these ideas because you'd like to see the existing decadent marketing power structure toppled (as I do) or because you'd like to exploit them for your own profit, you'll find this book an extremely entertaining and fruitful read.

> Mark Joyner
> Direct all hate mail to:
> http://www.MarkJoyner.name

Preface

I can tell you three things that the big ad agencies don't want you to know:

1. So-called "proprietary" branding schemes are all basically the same. *Proprietary* simply means they're using their own template. See page 43.

2. Agency-led client brainstorming sessions don't follow the basic guidelines for productive ideation. Creativity is learnable, and the basic tools are *not* used in most client sessions. See page 109.

3. Art directors and copywriters get raises, bonuses, and job offers when they win creative awards, *not* when you make money.

Here's the biggest secret you already know: Big agencies make money keeping this stuff complicated. That way you have to come to them.

In this book I give you tools to profit from these ideas. You will learn how to use big-agency tools without paying the big agency. And if you're hiring a big agency, learning these tools makes you less likely to be steamrolled by a five-dollar-word-spewing strategist or a chic Madison Avenue creative.

Branding is a dirty word to many business folks. Sure it is. They've been scorned, paying tons of money for ideas that weren't actionable and initiatives that cost more than they returned. That's not business. That's a hustle.

You shouldn't believe anything you're about to read. What follows is my perspective, based on my experience and recollections. You should not expect comparable results. I'm a lucky guy. Testing takes work. The harder I test, the luckier I get.

Test these ideas and discover what magic you can create. Magic is fun. Fun is magical. That much I know. For me, the rest is just a working hypothesis.

Welcome.

Introduction

As soon as possible, please buy a small notebook. This notebook will be your workbook for doing the exercises at the end of the chapters. Choose whatever kind of bound notebook you like. Mine happens to have graph paper, but traditionally lined or blank paper is fine. Regardless, I suggest you own a notebook dedicated to working on your branding ideas. I want you to be more profitable by the end of this book, and working on the exercises will help.

In the meantime, please write in this book. Use the margins and whatever space is available.

Thanks,

Ben

1

Pool Hall Wisdom

Marketing is like playing pool: You always have to be thinking two steps ahead. In pool, a player can keep playing so long as he sinks a ball. The real trick of the game is to *think two shots ahead*. When beginners start thinking not just of their next shot, but two shots out, they begin to see the game differently. What you're going to do next appears different when you begin to think two steps ahead. *Next* doesn't mean immediately; *next* simply means in the future.

You can take a real easy shot, and then what? Maybe you're stuck. When you think two shots ahead, you're planning to make a series of shots in a row, anticipating what's required to sink a few balls in a row. Maybe the shots work out as you plan, maybe you have to adjust, but I guarantee you that the more you practice thinking ahead, the more shots in a row you are likely to make.

Of course, you must have some basic skill at being able to shoot the cue ball and sink balls. You can think two shots ahead all you want, but if you can't sink a ball, your turn is still over.

If you are reading this marketing manual, I assume you're able to attract a customer and get a sale. Learning to make a sale is critical. This book is intended to help you grow your business. If you aren't thinking about what you're selling *next*, you aren't really marketing.

Getting the most out of each subsequent sale is a function of branding. I know the word *branding* is a total turnoff to many marketers. It's a dirty word to many CFOs. This bad reputation is often well deserved. Efforts in branding are often not only a sunk cost, but a lost cause. Branding is about maximizing what you make over the long haul and sustainably building your business. However, many branding consultants or brand managers act more like police than like profit-motivated business folks.

For instance, a few years ago I was working on Cingular at BBDO (Batten, Barton, Durstine & Osborn). We planned to spend $60,000,000 on advertising in one month, a disproportionately high budget for a month, but we were launching Rollover Minutes, a revolutionary pricing plan for wireless phones where unused minutes roll over to be used in later months. Part of the Rollover Minutes media plan included freestanding inserts (FSIs) for newspapers in most major and medium-size cities in America—about 80 million newspapers. Two weeks before the launch weekend there was an emergency: The color registration for nearly half these inserts was off, and there was discussion about not placing these FSIs for fear of tarnishing the brand's equity.

The shade of orange was not *that* important. What was important? A convenient way to learn the specifics about this revolutionary pricing plan, details to further explain how great Rollover Minutes really were. When it comes to saving money, I don't care that much about the color of the ink that teaches me how to save money.

In Chapter 2 we'll look at the widespread misinformation around the word *brand*. Then we'll set about defining the word *brand* in such a way that it will help us as marketers make more money. There are a lot of people who make a lot of money from being branding experts. It is in their interest to keep this knowledge secret. That's why they write in argot, the funky language that makes sense only to the people who live and breathe in that expertise. But before we go there, how about using what I gave you in this chapter? Try the following exercise, please.

EXERCISE 1

Write down the next two purchases your customer might make from you. Then detail what needs to happen for each of those purchases to take place.

_____

_____

_____

_____

_____

_____

Thank you. It's selfish of me to ask you do these exercises. I imagine that if you engage with these ideas then you are more likely to get value and share your experiences with friends. Why is this selfish? The more deeply you engage with this material the more likely you are to want my next product. The onus is on me to give you more value than you pay for. That's what will make you likely to want to keep doing business with me—you get more than you give. So please, give me a test-drive and scratch out an answer for this exercise.

If possible, you really should have a study partner. If you go into our forum you'll find folks working on this very exercise. You'll find our forum at www.ThinkTwoProductsAhead.com.

2

Brand Misinformation versus Back-End Thinking

Advertising is a seduction, not a debate.

—David Ogilvy

Branding is an extended seduction, not a color palette.

—Ben Mack

Branding is often discussed as irrelevant to small business marketing. That's bunk! If you are running a con-game, then branding is irrelevant. However, *every* form of legitimate business will benefit from branding. Branding is often described in absurd and outlandish ways.

For the record, **branding is *not***:

- an exact discipline.
- about always using the same logo or colors.
- about limiting yourself.

5

Don't use the dictionary for industry terminology. Most standard American dictionaries of the English language will define *brand* as "a trademark or proper name identifying a product, service, or manufacturer; a named product or product line, as in *a popular brand of shoes*." Please abandon this common definition of a brand. A doctor needs a medical definition of *manic*, or he would be prescribing everybody lithium. Marketers need a business definition of *brand*. Here's mine, from *Ben Mack's Dictionary of My Language*:

> **brand** 1. The positive or negative inclination to purchase, either in an individual or among a target audience. 2. The aggregation of stories and associations around a trademark, distinctive name or a product line. 3. (*vt*.) To increase a target audience's likelihood to purchase now and in the future. 4. To imbue positive characteristics into a marketed proposition. 5. (*Slang*) A colloquial word for a logo, product name or product line.

A brand is not a physical thing, but the relationship between consumers and a product or service. In this book, product names, product logos, and the products themselves are not brands. They are accessories to your relationship with a customer.

Few products really make a statement about their users. Products that carry a huge advertising budget can become a flag. What do I mean by a flag? Well, carrying a Heineken at a party is a flag that says you're sophisticated or, in dating terms, mature. Holding a Corona says relaxation, that you don't have an attitude—you're chillin'. The beer you drink says something about you—at minimum, it says you aren't an active member of Alcoholics Anonymous. (See Figure 2.1.)

Often I see the word *brand* bandied about as if it were synonymous with *logo*. Some brand managers treat their logo like a sacred flag. I saw a wrongly colored logo on a weekend sales brochure and the brand manager said they didn't want to use the brochures. They told me I would *never* hang an American flag with pink stripes instead of red, and

Figure 2.1 *You're probably not playing this kind of branding game.*

they were right—I wouldn't hang a pink American flag. I wouldn't buy a pink American flag. But we were selling fertilizer, not flags. I would have preferred that the color be perfect, but I would rather have the collateral selling my product than not have sales material.

This *flag* notion of branding works for huge-budget advertising, but it doesn't scale down to small businesses. For a flag to have meaning, folks must recognize and agree on, for example, what a Corona means, which requires a ton of advertising. Big-budget advertising can create meaning that is virtually impossible for small-budget marketers to garner outside of a very small niche audience. Corona becomes a flag that says, "I'm cool" but without using the word *cool*, and is seen as cool by a wide variety of people.

Flag branding, being able to turn your product or logo into a meaningful flag, is not a viable strategy for most advertisers. If you have that kind of budget, the rest of this book is important. But if you don't have anywhere near that kind of budget, then what follows is even more important, because every single contact you have with your dear customer is meaningful and can substantively affect your relationship and their likelihood to buy again.

If a customer or prospect interacts with your product or your communication and is more likely to buy your product or buy it again, you are building brand equity. This is often mistaken as *like-ability*. I have nothing against likeability—I just don't think it should be an overriding business objective. Remember that *nice* guy in your high school that all the girls *liked* but none of them slept with? He may have been liked but his brand equity was squat because he could never close the deal. When Ogilvy said that advertising is a seduction he was talking about getting laid, not endless flirting. If you aren't getting laid you aren't seducing your prospect. If you aren't getting sales you aren't building your brand—you're merely buying media.

I suggest you think of the word *brand* as the likelihood for a customer to do business with you *again*. In the next two chapters I discuss nurturing a relationship with somebody you'll never know personally. Then in Chapter 5 I show you how *all branding schemes are basically the same* and how to use these constructs to increase retention for big and small businesses. But I'm not finished discussing misinformation about branding.

Branding is big business. Millions of dollars of custom and syndicated research is sold in the name of brand planning. If somebody sold you research or a branding process that didn't generate more profit than it cost, I'm sorry. But don't throw the baby out with the bath water. There is value in branding, and there's also a ton of money wasted in the name of branding.

Before a client spends money on research I like to agree on what actions will be taken based on the possible findings. I trust sales data more than I trust most tracking studies that report awareness levels. Tracking studies are where target customers are polled at regular intervals to measure product awareness, awareness of advertising, or to discern who's considering your product. Neat, but I've rarely seen profitable steps taken from tracking data even when glaring insights were screaming to be used. A notable exception was working on

Mitsubishi with planning guru Jeffrey Blish. Usually, I see tracking data used to justify marketing inefficiencies. Our sales are down? The whole category is down! I've seen millions of dollars a year spent so that when sales go down somebody can reply with confidence that our sales dip is consistent with the category average.

Measuring metrics is how research companies make money—that's what they sell. Their primary job is to sell you on the importance and value of their research. When your advertising agency recommends a research company, chances are it is owned by the same holding company as your advertising agency. For instance, BBDO is owned by Omnicom. Omnicom owns over 300 communications companies, plus Diversified Agency Services (DAS). Never heard of DAS? It's the company that helps cross-sell clients between Omnicom companies. While I worked at BBDO, if I were to recommend three research vendors to a client, it was an unwritten expectation that at least two of them be Omnicom companies. The same with branding companies, and for good reason: If Cingular hired a branding company that wasn't an Omnicom company, they would likely undermine our efforts and elaborately detail exactly what we were doing wrong—making Cingular more likely to switch advertising agencies.

Even if the branding company is an independent and not out to undermine your ad agency, it will find problems with your brand. Why? Because if your brand is all-good, then they can't sell you any more services. Have you heard the expression "Never take your car to a bored mechanic"? A bored mechanic is hungry for work and thus more motivated to find things wrong with your car. Branding consultants get more money by finding things wrong with your brand so they can dive down into those issues and help you.

Research should be treated with skepticism. Research is an interpretive tool. After we launched the Rollover Minutes campaign, our second round of commercials featured a dance troupe that made music on a variety of props in an engaging way, with placards that

touted the value of Rollover Minutes. Our market share went up.
The ads worked. But the research company conducting the tracking
study, a company not owned by Omnicom, said this execution was a
waste of money—one of the worst ads for the wireless category in
recent years. I asked them to explain our increase in sales and increased market share. They said it was on the strength of the product
offering, of the Rollover Minutes themselves. Here's my take: The research was a telephone-interview study. The dance troupe had very
few words in the spot. When research participants were asked over
the phone if they recollected a TV commercial with dancers drum-
ming on unusual objects they said no.

Conversely, we had a spot with a cute dog that would roll over
every time the announcer said the word *rollover* in his voice-over.
This spot scored off the charts, according to their research method-
ology. The word *rollover* was said 17 times during a 30-second commercial. Customers remembered the commercial and stated over
the phone that it made them consider shopping Cingular. Despite
sales being flat, the research company released a press release stating
this was the best commercial the wireless category had seen in
years. Bunk! This spot just happened to test the best against their
measurements. We beat the test. We scored an A, but that didn't
make us money.

I'm skeptical of consultants with fancy formulas that derive
brand equity. I should know—I've been one of these consultants. I'm
registered to interpret data on Millard-Brown's BrandZ study, a proprietary approach to predicting the future sales of a line of branded
products, which is far better than most black-box methodologies, but
I wouldn't bet the farm on BrandZ results. I'm a huge fan of data but
often, general category studies give marketers as much data as they
will ever wisely use. If your sales are plummeting and it isn't a sea-
sonal deal, get hustling. I don't care what's happening to the rest of
the category.

When I started my own research company I eventually implemented a policy of charging $1,000 if I could talk a client out of research. I wasn't a great salesman. Often small companies would come to me wanting to invest $20,000 in four focus groups and I would talk them out of doing research. I still wanted to be compensated for my value, but many prospective clients would balk at this. So with those clients I became a great salesman: Whatever they said they were interested in is what I told them they needed. I stopped doing this because I couldn't charge them enough to compensate for my upset stomach.

Hiring a consultant can be a great way to get somebody else to do your homework. I've been that consultant. I've been doing other people's homework since the 8th grade at John Burroughs Jr. High School when Rachel of the Miller twins batted her eyes at me. Rachel, I've learned a couple things since I was 14. Next time I'll charge you.

The successful entrepreneurs I know don't view digging through data as work. They are driven to know, and understanding data is part of the process of knowing. They either enjoy understanding the underlying dynamics of their projects or they simply can't sleep if they don't understand something. In Chapter 3 we look at the interconnectedness of your equities and how to strengthen their relationships.

Branding is about planning your customer's experience, about thinking with the end in mind. Branding is often referred to as big picture planning, asking where are we now, really? Then, where can we be and how do we get there? However, in order to do this kind of planning we have to have a road map of the territory.

Figure 2.2 is a traditional purchase funnel. There are fewer and fewer customers the further down the funnel you go. If you are a Direct Response marketer (a term I coined with the help of David Garfinkel) this funnel changes, but arguably not that much.

Figure 2.2　*Traditional Purchase Funnel*

Let's start at the top with *Need*. If a customer doesn't "need" your product, they aren't considering paying you money. Some non-wealthy people get tripped up on the word *need*. They argue about the fine distinction between needs and wants. Okay, but I need to make money.

Some products and services create an awareness of the need that they solve. For example, Listerine popularized the word *halitosis*. Wisk laundry detergent made people aware of ring-around-the-collar. SafeCo wants you to know that if your auto is underinsured you could lose your house. This makes you reconsider your state of need. Are you underinsured?

The second level, *Aware*, is where a ton of money is wasted in the name of branding, for the sake of raising awareness. Don't get me

started on how raising awareness is
not a business objective in and of itself. I don't believe the formulas that
claim if you raise awareness to certain levels you'll achieve certain
sales. Bunk! Those formulas were
created by looking at successful
products that happened to have certain levels of awareness at certain
sales volumes.

However, awareness does help get you sales. Do they know your
name? More important, will they recognize you the next time they
are looking to spend money? Are they aware that your product fills a
need of theirs? Do they think of your product first? That's called top-
of-mind awareness. There's a proven correlation between top-of-
mind awareness and sales, but I see this working the other way. Top
businesses are often thought of first and afford enough communications to keep them top-of-mind.

The third level is *Consider*.
Have you ever considered buying
the Publix Premium Ice Cream?
I'll put their whole-bean vanilla up
against any vanilla. By contrast my
girlfriend, Liz Boswell, won't even
consider eating at Taco Bell. (I just
got kisses for working her name
into this.) Is your product/service
being considered by people as a

way of filling their need? The customer may know they have a
need; they may even be aware of your products. But are they considering you?

Arm & Hammer has mastered the art of inciting consideration
for using their baking soda for a plethora of occasions. Can you

smell anything in your fridge? It's time to use/replace your Arm & Hammer.

You don't choose whether or not you have a brand-you do have a brand. You choose whether you *manage* your brand. If somebody has bought from you once, are you exploiting future possibilities? *Exploit* means to use fully. That's an unachievable ideal. As marketers we should be considering how to leverage the future of our relationship with our customer. I'm hoping you'll buy from me in the future. Heck, I'm hoping you'll buy from me right now! Are you buying what I'm talking about? Showing why some buyers choose your offering can help other prospective buyers see their need.

Interested is the next level. Are you interested in learning more? Stoking the interest of your prospect is the role of branding. Direct Response letters are the epitome of stoking interest. Traditional branders would do well to heed their tactics.

Are you attractive? Remember, this is a seduction. For some folks, a modicum of formality is required. Do you know why your offering is attractive and to whom? For others, a formal voice would be staid and irrelevant. Every touch, every moment somebody spends with your product is part of your brand-your relationship. Is your relevance increasing or decreasing? Are you a pick-up artist prowling for a one-night stand, or do you want a relationship? Have I told you that I love you . . . recently?

Next we move to *Search*. If you're wooing a prospect and they go off searching—well, that *is* their prerogative. In fact, that's a great time for you to steal a customer somebody else has warmed up to a need that you can satisfy. But it works the other way, too. Your warmed prospect goes looking for other suitors. You can't directly control the

competition, and their interaction with
your customer affects your brand.

| Need |
| Aware |
| Consider |
| Interested |
| Search |
| Buy |
| Use |
| Prefer |
| Loyal |

What you *can* do is tell them
what to look for. Verizon boasts that
it has "the most reliable network."
This is calculated through some obtuse formula. Research studies have
shown that dropped calls are the most
annoying network failure, more an-
noying than no reception. Cingular has the fewest dropped calls.
When you're shopping for your next wireless phone, Cingular suggests you consider the frequency of dropped calls while you search.

I could win a beauty pageant if the qualifications for winning
were being 39, pudgy, and a business writer, having graying hair and
two or more middle names. I'd be a front-runner. If a prospect is going to go searching I hope you have told them what to look for that
will make you look good. Graying hair equals sophistication and experience. Are you ready to get down to business?

Marketing is a battle for share of wallet. In a retail store the dis-
play area is called point-of-purchase (POP). Online, this is your
web site. Direct Response marketers have this down cold. I'm
amazed that POP designers aren't attending Direct Response con-
ferences. But the real POP is the packaging. I think packaging
should be called BOP, for brink-of-purchasing. The packaging
should be closing the deal *and* reinforcing what a fine purchase
your customer has made.

The one thing you don't want them to search for is a way to
give you money. Can your prospects find you easily when they're
searching? How can you trump your competition? *Fewest dropped
calls* really undermines *most reliable network*. Where do your
prospects search out information to inform their purchase? Cell
phone buyers often search for deals in the Sunday paper. Giving
them a toll-free number is great. Having somebody there to answer

the phone on Sunday is even better. Otherwise, they may keep on searching.

Everything that comes into a consumer's mind about your product is part of your brand, but most of the message doesn't stick. Brands are bigger than advertising or your logo or any tangible. The logo and the brand name are physical manifestations of a brand, but they are not the brand; they are accessories, in the same way that a United States flag is not the United States.

The next step: *Buy*. Hallelujah! The interaction during the sale, the actual purchase, is part of the consumer's experience of your brand—a *big* part! Cadillac dealerships used to have a "staging" area for presenting the keys to the owner. Why did they call it a staging area? Because a Cadillac brand manager somewhere recognized the importance of celebrating the purchase and instilling both pride of ownership and a desire to have the buying experience again. Brilliant.

Recently, a friend bought a skateboard from a BMW dealership. It was a fancy Street Carver where the wheels hug the curves, and it is cool. But at the dealership my friend had to go through the same finance office as if he was buying a car, and this finance guy was peeved about selling a skateboard that he wasn't making money. When we left, my buddy said, "I never want to go through that again."

Whatever somebody is buying from you, I suggest you make buying from you a pleasure. Buying is a habit of theirs that you want to encourage. Moreover, it is a time when you can help the brand-new owner become a better user of your product. You can help them learn how to get an optimal experience from their ownership.

At point-of-purchase, how are you presenting yourself? What makes buyers choose you over the other guys? Is this in print someplace where the consumers are reading? Does your design instill a sense of confidence? Do you have inconsistencies undermining confidence in your product?

Now we come to *Use*. Orville Redenbacher told his patrons exactly how to pop his popcorn and they loved it. If you follow his instructions with other popcorn you get similar results. I've tried it. I'm not convinced his popcorn is so special. He sold branded instructions.

Can you better help customers like what they get? Can you help them appreciate their value? Are some customers happier than others? What's the difference between their experiences? Framing the customers' experience can help them better appreciate what actually happens.

If just one of these ideas sparks you, and implementing the idea increases repurchase by a modest 3 percent, what will that mean to your overall sales? What if tools to incite a second and third purchase allowed you to enjoy a 20 percent increase in sales? How much would that be worth to you?

Level eight is *Prefer*. So far, I haven't said anything that isn't essentially available in any number of books on sales and branding—I'm just saying it more simply. That's my goal, anyway, to have a conversation with you. I think a conversational tone is an easier way to learn than being lectured at. When I lecture, it sounds more like a rant.

I hope my writing is useful. I hope that in the future, if you are considering two books on a subject and I wrote one, you'll choose mine.

Bonding with a product is often best achieved through emotional connections, being real and sincere. There are other strategies, like exclusivity and elitism. That's more like fashion. Attitude can be fun, if you can consistently strike an emotional chord, but it is tough to keep up an act. Preference has more to do with emotional bonding than with functional benefits. I'm asking you to do a lot of hard work. I hope I'm making it fun.

Lastly, we come to *Loyal*. Now we're talking money. There are two basic types of loyal customers:

1. Loyal customers who will only buy from you when they have a need for the type of product you are selling.

2. Loyal customers who need everything you create.

If you are so blessed as to have either kind of loyal customers, please be nice to them. Few people can get away with continually attacking their loyal customer base. Creating a community around the loyal ones can help deepen the relationship. Community building is not something I can explain in great detail, because I haven't studied the phenomenon.

When I want to buy an apartment building I only use Jeff Lloyd of Horizon Realty, and he charges full commission. Anything Paul Auster writes, I'm buying. The same goes for Kurt Vonnegut, Neal Stephenson, John Carlton, and Mark Joyner. I've been waiting for Robert Anton Wilson's next book on Buckminster Fuller and memetics–I've been waiting with bated breath. I need Scope. Maybe it goes without saying, but I hope to become your new favorite author. I'm accessible and friendly and I like puppy dogs and long walks on the beach.

I've been studying Direct Response (DR) selling and copywriting for the past year. This book is my first venture into using DR. I'm learning hard-hitting sales techniques that are blowing my hair back. I'm getting professional help as I go along. I bought John Carlton's insider seminar. I'm working in trade with Mark Joyner and Michael Morgan. I'm partnering with Sam Heyer. My mantra is "Be the sponge." I watch, replicate, get feedback, test, refine, and repeat. I'm getting better. What fascinates me and endears these folks to me is a culture of learning, excellence, and fun.

Moreover, I like the scientific method they employ. The proof of a system is in the numbers. Are more people buying with strategy A or strategy B? It astounds me that more testing is not being employed in big-agency advertising. If you work at a big agency and take offense to my words, I'm sorry. I'm glad to know you *are* testing. However, when I worked in advertising, what we called testing often seemed absurd to me.

A real sales test happens while people are actually buying, not in sterile test center. Consumers vote with their dollars, and when their actual dollars aren't involved, I hold that only so much can be learned. Yes, pretesting is important to uncover confusion, but the testing shouldn't stop when the ad starts to run. I helped Marriott implement testing in their newspaper advertising. It was a revelation to them that they could test individual elements of an ad in real time.

I'm encouraging big-agency folks to buy my book, attend DR seminars, and get smarter about marketing. For a list of seminars to consider, please go to www.ThinkTwoProductsAhead.com/recommends/. Big-agency folks can learn a lot from Direct Response practitioners and other entrepreneurs.

But the reverse is also true: Entrepreneurs can learn a lot from what big agencies are doing. I hear some of the up-and-coming DR marketers using the word *brand* as a dirty word. As a branding practitioner I resemble their remarks and I don't care for the prideful ignorance disparaging my profession. Stop, please. There are things about big-agency advertising that many Direct Response practitioners can learn. I read many these ideas from the veteran world-class copy-writers. I find John Carlton's "Marketing Rebel Rant" (www .marketingrebelrant.com) chock-full of respect for the general principles of branding without using that word. The fact that John gives his rants away for free is a testament to his good will-panache, real style in prose and action. Thank you, John.

Now, many folks training new marketers are explaining a model that looks something like the one shown in Figure 2.3. The head-line must be intriguing to grab consumers' attention. You tease out their considerations, overcome their objections, and get the prospect really interested, and if all goes well they buy.

This is a great lesson. The skills and nuances discussed appear vast and substantial. Traditional advertisers would vastly improve their chops by taking a couple of your courses and actually doing the work.

Mastering the sale is imperative. Going on to the fancy stuff before you master the fundamentals is like attempting a bluff in poker

Figure 2.3 *Simplified Marketing Model*

before you really understand how to bet for value. I know the savvy practitioners of Direct Response see the profit in nurturing the lifetime value of customers. John Carlton explains:

> Far too many marketers are ungentlemanly cads. They high-five each other after the order is taken, and promptly move on to the next conquest. Big Mistake.
>
> That first order from your new customer is the initial round only. Your goal is to make them a customer for life—so you continue the bonding, reinforce their buying decision, and make them feel welcome, safe and warm in your arms.
>
> And sure, you're doing all that with your other customers, too.
>
> But as far as each individual knows, they are the only apple in your eye.
>
> *John Carlton, "Marketing Rebel Rant" 12 (May 2003),*
> *www.MarketingRebelRant.com.*

As Figure 2.4 shows, it's a continuing cycle of nurturing loyalty by eliciting their desire to buy from you.

What I hear John illuminating is that the sale is not the endgame. Your sale is really the beginning of a sustainable business

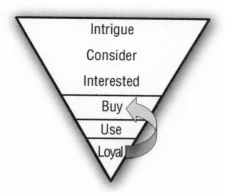

Figure 2.4 *Nurture the Lifetime Value of Customers*

relationship, an extended seduction that reinforces your appreciation of the customer's patronage.

Buy, use, appreciate results, buy again. Buy, use, appreciate. Guide them to buy, help them use your product for maximum effect, help them appreciate the results/experience they have, suggest their next purchase. This is your path to loyalty.

Figure 2.5 demonstrates what an information marketer's purchase funnel looks like.

Internet marketing master Mike Filsaime (www.Butterfly Marketing.com) says, "My big strides in income came when I started to understand that you can not make huge money with $47 ebooks. A small percentage will do it, but there is still money left on the table unless you create a back end." Branding is about setting up your back end. You don't want to just make a sale, you want to make several sales in a row to the same customer. You want to think two products ahead. You want your customer to crave your next product. This is an endless seduction. Need inspiration? Watch the movie *50 First Dates*. You are constantly seducing your customer and demonstrating why they love you and need more of you *right now*.

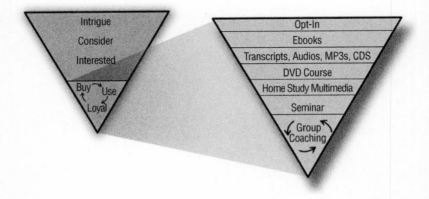

Figure 2.5   *An Information Marketer's Purchase Funnel*

In the next chapter we look at how Deutsch Advertising really cracked the code of integrating hard–selling tactics in ads that reinforced an overall appeal for a mass product. *Selling hard* and *branding* are not mutually exclusive.

But first I'm going to ask you to take stock of your real estate and your equities.

1. Write down every touch a customer has with your product—from packaging to web site to your phone message.

_____

_____

_____

2. In what ways might your packaging and ancillary real estate reinforce the value of using your products?

_____

_____

_____

3. Write down every proper noun you use, such as product names.

_____

_____

_____

3

The Common Thread and *Thinking* Two Products *Ahead*

A satisfied customer is the beginning of brand equity. Satisfying her a second time is more profitable. Branding is the process of repeatedly satisfying your customer, uncovering the heart of her satisfaction and consistently delivering both products and messages that frame and fulfill her expectation of satisfaction.

What's the common thread of her satisfied experience? Once you identify this common thread, your brand essence, you can prominently weave this thread into your communications and create products that specifically satisfy this commonality.

Let's say you sell Elvis paraphernalia and rare documents about Elvis and Graceland. "Elvis" is not your common thread; "love for Elvis" is likely your common thread. Many of your customers would surely be put off if you sold anything that denigrated Elvis.

Wells Fargo Case Study

A hundred years ago, mentioning Wells Fargo would conjure an image of a stagecoach delivering packages. Remember the play, *The Music Man*, where the whole town sings in anticipation of the cool stuff that might be delivered to them via the Wells Fargo wagon? Wells Fargo was the UPS of the second half of the nineteenth century. Wells Fargo was a company to be trusted with valuables. While Wells Fargo has always offered certain banking services, it was best known for its transportation services.

In 1918, the federal government assumed operations of the nation's railroads and express services as a wartime measure. Wells Fargo, American Express, Southern Express, and all other express companies' offices, equipment, and employees were merged into one vast American Railway Express. However, Wells Fargo continued its banking business independently. Wells Fargo was successful because of the strength of its brand—customers trusted Wells Fargo with their valuables so they trusted Wells Fargo with their money.

What was their common thread? Wells Fargo provided safety for valuables.

Today, when you need a company you can trust with your money, you may consider Wells Fargo. Trust is the essence of Wells Fargo's brand, more than its physical banks, checks, or even its name. The name became a symbol of this trust, but without this trust, the company would have evaporated when the government took over Wells Fargo's express business. It was the customers' willingness to do business with Wells Fargo that allowed it to continue when the business suddenly had to switch product offerings. It was the business managers leveraging Wells Fargo's common thread that facilitated the company finding new business opportunities.

Some people would argue that what I just described is just plain marketing. Maybe. But discussions around brand generally have to do with equity, while discussions around marketing have to do with specific transactions. Because brand equity is difficult or impossible to quantify exactly, some say it doesn't exist. I know *brand equity is real*. Premium brands charge premium prices and sell great volumes of products. Just go into your grocery store and look around; you'll notice that generic or store-labeled products are less expensive than nationally advertised products, even on commodities like salt or sugar. The packaging is sometimes better, making the container easier to pour or seal, but there's something else going on there.

Brands can create magic. What I mean by *magic* is something extraordinarily special. It just makes us feel good. Brands that sell fashion and cosmetics are exquisite in their ability to make us feel good. Managing your brand will help prevent your products from going out of fashion. However, I won't be discussing brands primarily sold in fashion magazines. Fashion is as much about breaking rules as it is about adhering to what's popular. I'm not an expert on fashion—I leave that to my girlfriend and I will wear what she tells me to, just like I let an art director design my book covers. I don't know how to make that kind of magic—but I know how to guide them.

You don't have a choice whether you want a brand, only whether you're going to manage it. Where do brands come from? The stork brings them! I'm joking. Brands manifest wherever business is done. Do you want to do business with that person again? Even swap meets have branding issues. In San Bernardino, California, I saw a new swap meet that advertised "Friendlier Vendors." Friendlier vendors than where? Friendlier vendors than the old swap meet a few miles away. This swap meet learned that shoppers wanted a friendly buying experience.

In today's consumer economy, *shopping is fun*. What is the number one activity to do while on vacation? It's not golf, it's shopping! (Grocery shopping is an exception to the maxim that shopping is fun, with the possible exception of Publix, where "Shopping is a pleasure.") Even bargain hunting at a swap meet is affected by branding, because branding is not the design of the logo but the experience. The experience of buying affects my likelihood to buy again or even consider buying again.

Brands manifest wherever business is done, and they are stewarded through the help of a *brand vision*. Brand visions are handmade by marketers and executives, but brands are disseminated by every touch consumers have with any context of your brand. A brand vision is not nearly as complicated nor as ethereal as often described. I'm going to make creating a brand vision real simple for you.

Names, logos, web sites, and packaging are invitations to enjoy your product or service, to do business with you. Every contact a consumer has with your company should be inviting—an extension of your hospitality and an invitation to buy now.

Until the mid-1990s, there were two primary types of TV commercials for automobiles:

1. National brand spots
2. Dealer retail spots

Automobile dealerships pay money for advertising into two kitties, a national fund and a regional fund. It used to be that the national fund was for brand advertising created by the manufacturer and run through national media. The regional fund was for retail advertising created by a local dealer association and run through that region's media.

Brand advertising was good at raising perceived esteem for an automobile or line of automobiles but did little good for generating immediate sales. While retail advertising would stimulate immediate sales, it actually undermined the overall opinion of consumers not currently shopping for vehicles. The mind-set of the shopper is very different from the mind-set of the user. A shopper hears a sale as "good value" while a user often hears the same message as "cheap."

In the left half of Figure 3.1 you can see "Opinion" and "Con-

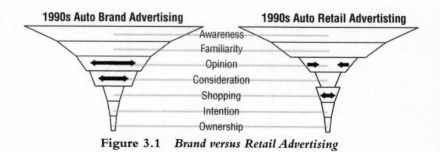

Figure 3.1 *Brand versus Retail Advertising*

sideration" broaden while the old brand ads ran, but they did very little to drive immediate traffic on showroom floors. However, the diagram on the right shows that dealer retail ads, extolling people to "come on in, today we're offering . . . ," hurt people's "Opinion" of the car and their future "Consideration" for the car went down as well. So car companies used to alternate between local/regional retail ads and national brand ads.

It took a long time for advertising folks to figure out how to build a brand and drive retail at the same time. Don't be too harsh on advertisers. We got to the moon and back before we figured out how to put wheels on a suitcase. Remember suitcases before Travel Pro? Technology evolves and only in hindsight do we say it was obvious.

Automobile ads today often do both well: They improve the public's overall opinion of a car while generating an immediate interest in those who are shopping. What used to be called brand spots are part of what contributed to some of the misnomers of branding today. Many creative ad writers used to pride themselves on not selling in national brand spots. Not much of this sentiment has survived in advertising. Why? Because branding is about making money! This is business.

The challenge cracked was to stimulate immediate sales while building the positive image of the product. When I worked at Deutsch Advertising in 1996 I saw them crack this advertising puzzle with Eric Hirschberg's work on Mitsubishi automobiles. The brand essence of Mitsubishi was vitality, and there was a common thread of verve through all their communications. Deutsch created a promotion with the theme of "Wake up and drive." All national spots drove a retailing message as they communicated an essence of vitality. In one message they increased future consideration for Mitsubishi and drove immediate traffic to the salesroom floor.

Your business is healthy when people are both buying now *and* intending, or at least open, to buy in the future.

Branding is nurturing *your* golden goose that lays *your* golden eggs. How do you nurture your golden goose? Be good to your gander. I'll explain this in the next chapter.

1. Write an exhaustive list of why people give you money—in other words, their reasons for buying.

_____

_____

_____

_____

_____

_____

2. Write down the emotional benefit behind each of these reasons for buying.

_____

_____

_____

3. Write down a different emotional benefit for purchasing your product

_____

_____

_____

For example, let's say you sell automobile insurance. Here's how you might answer these three questions:

Why They Buy	Emotional Benefit	Another Emotional Benefit
Legally required	Peace of mind	Easy—I make it easy to buy
Protect car	Confidence	Well rested—they can sleep without worry
Protect house	Being responsible	Love of family

Keep raising the stakes and see what emerges. If you don't have enough auto insurance, and you get in a bad enough wreck, a plaintiff can go after your house. Getting adequate auto coverage is an expression of your love for your family. If you think this is B.S., speak to somebody who lost their house because they were inadequately covered.

Keep this real, but keep raising the stakes. What are you *really* providing?

As another example, let's say you sell cell phones. You might answer the questions like this:

Why They Buy	Emotional Benefit	Another Emotional Benefit
Need it for work	Feeling productive	Empowerment
In case of emergency	Confidence	Feeling calm
Reachable by friends	Aware, in the know	Enfranchised—part of community
Stay connected with spouse, kids	Connection	Love of family

In the mid 1990s, cell phone ads were all about productivity and empowerment. Then ads started to discuss the upside to having a cell phone for an emergency. Now it's more about humanity and friends or the network. Love is a big seller—family packs are sold around holidays.

Your list of reasons to buy should be as long as you can make it. Don't worry about repeating emotional benefits or leaving blanks. This will be helpful when you extract your brand essence. Can you discover a common thread that encompasses your strongest emotional benefits? What would you love to help your customer accomplish?

4

Branding?
Be Good to
Your Gander

Sales is about identifying a thirsty prospect and selling them a glass of water. Branding is about selling them the second glass and the third glass and the fourth until when they're thirsty they want to buy your water. Ultimately, you want everybody to feel deprived if they can't have your water.

If a brand is a relationship between consumers and a named product or service, then branding is nurturing this relationship. *Branding* is the process of connecting with consumers and creating continuity between your products, so that customers want to buy your product now and will want to buy your product in the future.

Isn't marketing the same thing as branding? Yes, when it's good. Marketing tends to focus on *what* you say *where*; branding tends to focus on *how* you say *what*. Marketing and branding are interdependent.

Branding is about making money. Branding is about identifying what is attracting customers to buy your product, your common thread, and weaving this thread into your product and communications as fully and authentically as possible.

If branding is nurturing your golden goose, how do you do that? The most fabulous brand in the world is worthless without a customer. You know that a goose can't lay a fertile egg without a gander, a male goose. You've heard the expression, "What's good for the goose is good for the gander." Well, it works the other way, too. So be good to your gander. Be good to your customer. Love and respect your profitable customer. Without a customer your goose can't lay those golden eggs.

Thinking two products ahead will help you attract the appropriate gander. The most expensive part of marketing is getting a new customer—but what kind of customer? You want a profitable customer. Sales can be a great way to get rid of aging merchandise to end-using customers, but it is usually a lousy way of fertilizing your golden goose.

Allow me to address this in a roundabout way. In advertising I've worked as an account planner or a brand strategist. What's the difference? I don't know. What I do know is that highly successful ad agencies often refer to an account planner as a consumer advocate, but I have never heard that phrase in shops that called me a brand strategist. Many businesses would be more profitable if they hired consumer advocates, people to speak up when the company is about to upset or disappoint its customers.

While I was working with the Baskin-Robbins account, we were promoting a two-scoop sundae for $1.99. The image shown in Figure 4.1 is not the actual product we were promoting but an image I purchased from istock.com. However, each of the ice cream scoops here appears to be a 2.5-ounce scoop of delicious ice cream.

The problem with our promotion was that franchisees weren't making much money on these sundaes with the customary five ounces of scrumptious ice cream. So corporate decided to appease these

Figure 4.1   *A Two-Scoop Sundae*

owners by authorizing the use of one 2.5-ounce scoop and one 1.5-ounce scoop. I pointed out that our customers wouldn't really be experiencing our Baskin-Robbins Two-Scoop Sundae. They said they would train in-store employees to explain to customers that this was a trial size.

That seemed impractical and, sure enough, it flopped. For a time it seemed like everybody was happy—customers flocked in, franchisee owners and corporate were all happy. But when the sale ended the customers evaporated. The regular price of $2.99 wasn't attractive for what they had experienced. It might have been, had the sale product been a full serving, but that hypothesis would have required testing to validate. Perhaps creating a new name for this smaller size product would have been a more sustainable strategy.

In a later meeting it was suggested that maybe if the advertising showed the product from the proper angle we could only give the customer two 1.5-ounce scoops. I replied, "Maybe if the advertising is really good enough, and we trained the store employees well enough, we could get folks to come in and give us their money and wouldn't need to give them any ice cream at all." That didn't go over so well. Lines like that are part of I'm a better freelancer than employee. But I digress. There was no strategy! Furthermore, there was no love. They were looking at their customer impersonally, as in Figure 4.2.

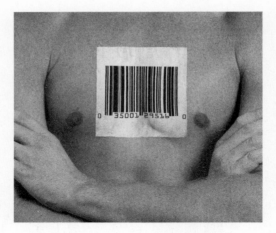

Figure 4.2 *Just Another Customer*

Let's say our new customers just love that $1.99 two-scoop sundae, which they did. Now what? There was no plan for transferring this behavior, nor for extending the product they grew to love. There was no thinking two products ahead. There was only thinking about driving immediate sales.

Branding is about keeping your new customers while you attract more customers. That sounds basic, but it seems to be extraordinarily rare in practice. And maybe this is just basic marketing—so I want to talk about magic.

Sometimes branding is magic. Are you old enough to remember this: In the 1980s, Wendy's had bigger hamburgers than most other fast-food joints, what in the industry are called quick service restaurants. Wendy's unique selling point was bigger burgers. Branding asked, "How do we say we have bigger burgers?" Their marketers agreed to their ad agency's solution of an old woman asking of the competitions' burgers, "Where's the beef?!" Great ad. Sales went up.

Sales didn't stay up. Sure, Wendy's is doing fine—but they had some magic and they let the magic slip away.

What am I talking about? "Where's the beef?!" They were promising a bigger burger. They were promising *big*. Now, 20 years later, you can see remnants of this notion on their menu in their Biggie® drinks and fries, and people still remember this phrase, but Wendy's isn't known for "big" today, not really. The $6 hamburger and other choices have become the Hummer of fast-food burgers.

Branding is finding out what you stand for, and then communicating and delivering what you stand for.

Here's why the magic works. Modern consumers suffer from constant *overchoice*—they have too many things to choose between. In a supermarket, I'm confronted with 14 different brands of barbecue sauce in nine different flavors. I never look at all my choices. Last week I was asked to bring some to a friend's house so I got a gourmet one. If it were for my own chicken, I'd start by looking at what's on sale. But whatever the case is, I start narrowing my choices.

Studies have shown that people who claim "I always buy what's on sale or the lowest price item" are liars. Maybe *lying* is too harsh—nobody died because of their reporting error. When their carts were analyzed, 80 percent of these people had more than half of their cart filled with products that were neither on sale nor the lowest price.

How does this happen? Overchoice. We don't like to think *too much*.

We buy what we bought last time. We like some products more than others. Sure, many of us play Sudoku, solve crossword puzzles, or play video games like Myst, but that's fun thinking, time we set aside for problem solving. In a supermarket customers aren't scrutinizing their choices for an optimal score, but getting through the chore of grocery shopping.

We don't like to think. Why is this important? In most cases, consumers limit their consideration to the products that are familiar in some way. *We like what we already know.* Further studies have shown that these consumers sometimes literally don't see products that they aren't familiar with. When presented with overchoice we *see only what we already know.*

Part of leveraging branding is to present yourself consistently, showing customers that you're already familiar. Why are bad-acting celebrities valuable? They are already familiar. In an attention econ-omy, recognition is valuable. Leverage your recognition; leverage your desirability.

Branding is consistently communicating and delivering what you stand for in a profitable way. Branding is like poker—the level of the stakes affects the nature of the game. Most of the books on branding discuss high-stakes branding with multimillion-dollar ad-vertising campaigns. I've played this game. I'm not very good at the politics. But what I found were great tools for opening new doors to perceiving brands differently, and I'm revealing them in this book. I'm not breaking any nondisclosure agreements because I discovered an underlying similarity in approaches.

It doesn't matter what stakes poker you are playing, in any casino in the world a full house always beats a flush, but not a royal flush. Just like poker, branding involves a lot of luck. However, in both poker and branding the high-stakes pros have developed tools to minimize risk and exploit advantages.

What I hope to do in the next chapter is make the multimillion-dollar tools accessible to lower-stakes branding practitioners. Candidly, I imagine lower-stakes branding practitioners will make better use of this material: You're playing with your own money and you take profits far more seriously than a politician does. (I see most corporate execu-tives as being more like politicians than truly business folks.)

These tools may appear too simple to be useful. I beg to differ. Claw hammers may not look glamorous, but if you had sold them to craftsmen 100 years ago you could have made a fortune. When a crafts-man uses a better tool, he sees it makes his work easier and faster, and the result is a stronger product. Imagine the pride you will feel the first time you hear a competitor say, "I wish I had thought of that."

Any sufficiently advanced technology is indistinguishable from magic.
—Arthur C. Clarke,
in *Profiles of the Future*, Clarke's third law

1. Take your emotional benefits from the previous chapter and write them on index cards. Lay them out in front of you. What kinds of groupings do you see? Name these groupings by picking a word that reflects the content of each grouping.

_____

_____

_____

2. Look at these names. Is there a label that would encapsulate these ideas? Write down whatever comes to mind and continue on. Don't get stuck on any of these exercises.

_____

_____

_____

_____

_____

5 | Branding Processes Are Strikingly Similar

I've worked at seven ad agencies—big ones like BBDO, Deutsch, and JWT, and boutiques such as WongDoody and TG Madison— each with its own proprietary branding process. Yet they're *all* doing the same thing. I'm not alone in this perception. Here's a quote from a man who's a bigwig in helping companies find new ad agencies:

> It should come as no surprise that the mechanics of most so-called proprietary branding processes are startlingly similar.
>
> *Mike Agate, chairman and founder of Select Resources International,*
> *in his December 2001 newsletter*

Marketing companies may use different words in their branding scheme, with different labels and pictures, but virtually all of them use the same three steps, shown in Figure 5.1.

That term in the center, *Brand Essence*, refers to a handle that you create to describe the *relevance* that compels people to want to give

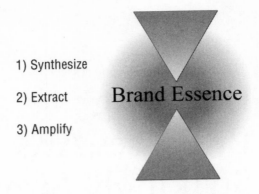

1) Synthesize

2) Extract

3) Amplify

Brand Essence

Figure 5.1   *Three Steps in Branding*

you their money. This is your common thread. It is difficult to reduce all your relevance into one word, or even two or three words, but it is useful in making your communications feel integrated.

My brand essence is "Debunking Consensus Reality." That's really clunky and uses some big words, and that's fine. A brand essence need only make sense to the marketing team. I also use "Residual Streams of Income" as sub–brand essence. How does this work? Most businesspeople are looking to make sales; asking marketers to think two sales ahead and create product pathways that manifest residual streams of income appears to me as a form of debunking consensus reality. I see this as reinforcing my overarching brand essence because I'm altering your take on normality and reality. Your brand essence needs to be clear to the folks helping you craft your communications.

In 2001 when I worked with Clif Bar, their brand essence was "Mojo"—that's an extreme case of a loose definition, but it worked for the Clif Bar team. Something similar works for the luxury women's undergarment company Spanx. Until you have a multimillion-dollar company, I suggest you choose a more tangible brand essence. Your goal is to have something that enables you to ask yourself, concerning any activity you might consider: "Does this activity reinforce a sense of (fill in your brand essence)?"

That's it. That's the $197 idea. I know, this doesn't seem like it's worth that much, yet. The rest of this book is an instruction manual on using this $197 idea. If you think $197 is a lot of money, you are playing low-stakes business. At BBDO I had an opportunity to look at the final PowerPoint for a global positioning project for Pepsi. I think they paid over $10,000,000 for an answer, and it was a one-word answer—not yes or no, but a one-word encapsulation of their positioning: "More." You don't remember hearing the word *more* repeated ad nauseam in their commercials? That's because *more* was the essence they were communicating—*not the word*. Repeat: Your brand essence is not the word(s) necessarily used in your communications.

Let's see how this works: Does *Think Two Products Ahead* reinforce a sense of debunking consensus reality? I hope so. My brand essence, "Debunking Consensus Reality," basically means "dispelling popular myths." Branding is often made to appear complicated. Many marketers coming across discussions on branding find the topic irrelevant and costly. I'm making a case that branding is understandable, relevant, and most importantly, *profitable*.

Does (insert a Pepsi communication) reinforce a sense of "More"? If it doesn't, then they look for another communication. This idea helped Pepsi reflect the desires of their identified target audience in an easy to understand, relevant, and most importantly, *profitable* way.

But you can't really *profitably* use this tool until you extract your brand essence. So, back to explaining the branding process . . .

Sometimes an illustration of a branding process is turned horizontally. Often, the amplification phase is a rainbow, as if the brand essence is a prism through which communications are projected. Another way of saying this is that your brand essence is the common thread that must be woven through all your communications. When you look at a communication, ask yourself if it feels like it was cut from the same cloth as the rest of your communications.

Figure 5.2 provides another visual depiction of the same process.

Ideally, a brand essence remains virtually unchanged from one

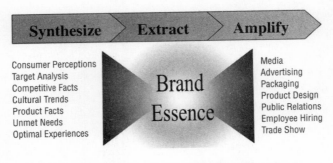

Figure 5.2   *Another View of the Branding Process*

decade to the next. You can see the thread of your brand over the ages and woven into every communication. The advertising and packaging of your brand may change, but a true brand essence remains constant. I haven't worked on Betty Crocker, but I imagine their brand essence is "Love on the Table." Now, the image of Betty Crocker herself needs to shift with changing fashion, but the essence that baking is a sign of love remains constant.

Synthesizing means analyzing everything you know about your target, your product, and your competition. You can spend thousands of hours and millions of dollars doing this phase, but this phase is not what a customer is truly buying. Pepsi paid over $10,000,000 because they needed the research in order to land on "More" with confidence.

What is this magical brand essence? Yes, I truly do believe it is magical. (No, I don't want hate mail from readers telling me that mentioning the word *magic* is likely to condemn me to eternal damnation. I appreciate your desire to help; now go check out GetForgiven.com.)

Figure 5.3 gives a quick review of marketing. Arguably, this diagram is not drawn to scale. In reality your product probably barely overlaps with the customer's life concerns. Even if your product feeds a passion like golf or making money, your product is only relevant to a sliver of a customer's overall life.

Now we're getting into the thick of synthesis and positioning

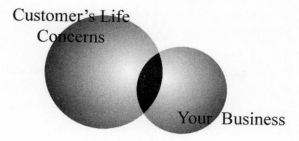

Talk about the stuff that overlaps, but which stuff do you talk about?

Figure 5.3 *Marketing Highlights the Connection between Your Business and Your Customer*

considerations. This is where your work begins. Do you have your notebook handy? You should be writing down whatever appears valuable to you. This is a workbook. Write on these pages. What I share next is the prep work I go through before I work with a client on their branding. It is better to write down an idea you don't use than to remember you had an idea and then not be able to recollect what the notion was. The first word of the title of this book is *Think*. I'm helping you think about profitable thinking.

We're delving into how to slice and dice ideas. These are likely to be new skills to you. If at first you don't find them easy, keep working. Like most things in life, they get easier with practice. If positioning were too easy, people like me couldn't charge a couple grand a day for our services—and that's the wholesale price. Some folks charge substantially more. Similar to other disciplines, practice helps.

The best I've ever seen is Andrew Robertson, CEO of BBDO Worldwide. While I know many pitfalls to working with big agencies, they also have the budgets to hire some of the best talent. I'd like to work with Kevin Roberts, CEO of Saatchi & Saatchi. His book *Lovemarks* makes complete sense to me. However, the tactics illustrated may be difficult for some marketers to scale down for smaller brands. Roberts explains the value of finding a brand's love story and transforming their logo into a Lovemark. Brilliant.

Ideally, a brand essence remains virtually unchanged from one decade to the next. The advertising and packaging of your brand may change to stay contemporary, but a true brand essence remains constant. Part of stewarding the brand is championing the brand essence. If your corporate culture is confused or conflicted on your brand essence, it is time to either regroup and address current concerns, or go through a branding process. Be as wary of changing your brand essence as our government is of altering the Constitution: We have added amendments, but each amendment has been exhaustively explored and debated before ratification.

Every dollar you spend on developing your brand is a dollar that is not going toward communicating with your target. Why invest in uncovering your brand essence? Investing in defining your brand can make your media dollars go further, because each message becomes more efficient and all of your messages work stronger in concert. You get a concerted effort. This effect works in mass marketing and one-to-one marketing. Whether you're advertising on TV or selling one at a time with direct response letters, your product should reflect your pitch so the customer feels satisfied and will be excited to do business with you again.

How much can your company invest? Large companies often retain a branding firm to help them articulate their positioning and brand promise. The total cost of this service can easily exceed $250,000, often costing millions of dollars. The advertising agencies of these companies may be able to yield comparable results utilizing similar processes for a fraction of this cost. Sometimes they can't. It's similar to getting a paint job for your car; you can spend however much you want. At the end of the day, a $249 paint job and a $28,000 paint job both yield a red car that basically looks the same from 10 feet away.

The more you spend, the less discernable the difference. The distinction between a $2,000 paint job and a $6,000 paint job may take a trained eye to discern. The difference between a $6,000 paint job and a $28,000 paint job may entail disassembling the car to appreciate these differences. However, some companies won't have confidence in the branding process without a certain level of expenditure. Spending too little will undermine the value to some buyers.

I learned that lesson the hard way. When I was 19, I was paying my way through UCLA as a magician. I was performing at RJ's for Ribs in Beverly Hills on Saturday nights. A woman from San Francisco asked me what I would charge, above expenses, to perform at a party in Northern California. I said a thousand dollars, more than twice what I had ever charged for a show up to that point. Two weeks later she got back to me and said that she and her husband had gotten into a fight over it. She really wanted me, but her husband held to "What kind of a magician are we going to get for only a thousand dollars?"

Obviously, a local florist shouldn't spend $250,000 on articulating its positioning and brand essence. But the processes covered in these chapters are still relevant. A single store may conduct consumer research by talking directly to its clients, as opposed to conducting focus groups in several markets.

It is irresponsible for a nationally advertised brand not to invest a certain amount annually in consumer research to understand shifts in consumer perceptions and to implement these findings as they maintain the relevance of their brand's voice. Hopefully, this book will help you gauge an appropriate level of spending. If you call a branding company or call a branding consultant and ask them if you need to do a comprehensive brand assessment, they will respond with a resounding "Yes!" Branding consultants are salespeople. They make money by selling their services. You may not need all their services. You may be able to take certain tasks off their plate.

Please don't misconstrue this commentary. I am not advocating spending the least amount of money possible. Doing bad consumer research is far worse than doing no research at all. Getting bad branding advice is far worse than figuring it out for yourself. It is much better to find that something costs more than you thought it would, than to discover that you spent less than you should have. If you speak with five different branding firms, chances are you will hear five different proprietary methods for branding, each of them claiming to be "the best of the best of the best." Some of these methods will utilize a metaphor, where the phases of the project get labeled like some familiar process. Others may have a theme, and the way they name the phases relates to that theme. Other branding schemes may label their phases by the function of each phase. Which one's best? The one that makes the most sense to you, and the one where the people you will be working with seem like people you *can* work with. Make sure you meet the people with whom you will actually be working with on a day-to-day basis.

Ask about your bid. If you need a lower bid, ask in what ways they might be able to lower this cost, and ask what you would sacrifice. Perhaps existing research can replace a portion of the proposed initial research. It may be that you can pay this branding partner to synthesize some of your recent research instead of commissioning new studies. You may be able to synthesize some of the research for the vendor. Saving them time should save you money. However, it may be that they need to conduct the research they propose in order to do the job the way they feel it needs to be done.

A warning about reducing costs: It is usually better to spend more than you originally budgeted than to go forward and find that you spent less than you really needed to. I've worked on too many research studies where we lowered the sample size in order to reduce costs and garnered inconclusive findings. In those cases, a lot of money was spent and not much could be done with confidence.

In the next chapter we start our mental calisthenics. The processes I explain are not the final product. Customers don't buy your marketing positioning statement. However, not doing these kinds of exercises lessens your likelihood of consistently resonating with your customer and nurturing your golden goose.

You need a gut–check. If all the pieces of a puzzle fit together but there isn't any soul to your communications, it probably won't really resonate with your prospects or your current customers, either. There are other marketers seeking to woo your customers away. Be beautiful.

> *When I'm working on a problem, I never think about beauty. I think only how to solve the problem. But when I have finished, if the solution is not beautiful, I know it is wrong.*
>
>   —R. Buckminster Fuller

EXERCISE 5

1. Look at your product and packaging: Has as much thought gone into this as went into your sales and marketing material? Does your packaging reinforce what you touted in the marketing of your product? If your product and packaging were marketing another product, would it be different?

2. If you are looking for books on leveraging your brand essence, please consider reading *The Culture Code* by Clotaire Rapaille (New York: Broadway Books, 2006). Dr. Rapaille explains how he extrapolates a "culture code" for a product or category. A culture code can then be used as a brand essence in that all communications should be reinforcing this notion. For a complete list of books I recommend on branding, persuasion, and entrepreneurial life skills, please go to www.ThinkTwoProductsAhead.com/Recommend.

6

What's a Brand Essence?

Your brand essence is a mental territory where you have an advantage. You selected this common thread because it empowered your sales. Framing is about what you bring to the forefront of your customer's mind. If you revisit your list of possible framings, please add to your list.

We've been synthesizing data—damn, that looks like a complicated concept, synthesizing data, but that's what we've been doing. Hopefully three things have happened in the process:

1. A few cool things have emerged.
2. You have some new perspectives.
3. You are developing a new relationship with cohesive ideas.

We're getting ready to extract a brand essence. Let's revisit the depiction of this process from the previous chapter (see Figure 6.1).

Ideally, a brand essence remains virtually unchanged from one decade to the next. The advertising and packaging of your brand may

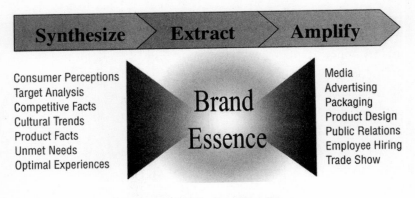

Figure 6.1   *The Branding Process*

change, but a true brand essence remains constant. I know I said that earlier, but most brand managers get caught up with the functionality of their products without seeing the bigger picture of their brand essence.

Sergio Zyman uses the term *core essence* instead of brand essence. Fine—same difference. Zyman suggests that understanding how your core essence is relevant now and how it is becoming relevant is the heart of sustainable business:

> You may think you're innovating, but you're probably just wasting money. Try renovating instead. . . . A recent disaster is the Walkman. While Sony was busy making colorful new versions of personal, portable CD players, Apple was out there redefining portable entertainment. Sony should have introduced iPods, not Apple. So what was the domain of Sony is now Apple's forever.
>
> *Sergio Zyman, "The Innovation Illusion,"*
> CMO Magazine, *February 26, 2006*

Your essence is what you're building and reinforcing.

The biggest choice in extracting a brand essence is choosing whether your brand essence should be tangible or intangible. Tangible essences tend to be about physical attributes such as low prices (e.g., Wal-Mart, SouthWest) or large size (e.g., Amazon, Star Network ATMs), while intangible brand essences are experiential, like luxury (e.g., Rolex, Mount Blanc) or relaxation (e.g., Corona, Levis).

Before you go mucking with your image, start by asking what has been the key to your success so far? Is this key sustainable? Is there a damn good reason that this key to your success shouldn't be your brand essence? Just checking. If you are new to this idea of a brand essence, think about what has been your key to success. Now how does that feel to the customer. What's the consumer's benefit?

Be wary of broadening your definition of your brand essence. In the 1970s, Miller Beer owned relaxation: "It's Miller Time." Miller broadened their essence to include the beer that buddies share. This left relaxation undefended. Today, Corona stands for relaxation. Miller stands for what exactly?

The objective of extraction is to create a platform that leverages the favorable conditions identified during synthesis. This is a battle for a mind and you want to engage on the most advantageous terrain.

> Military strategists know that most battles are won before the first shot is fired—by the side that determines where, when and how an engagement is fought. . . . Political professionals call the act of defining the terrain of engagement "framing the debate."
>
> *James Carville and Paul Begala,* Buck Up, Suck Up
> *(New York: Simon & Schuster, 2003)*

In branding, your essence is your terrain. Your essence should be a ground where, if you were challenged, you would likely win.

I argue that once a brand essence is identified, the company should structure itself around delivering that brand essence. A brand essence needs to be more than communication talk points. A brand essence needs to be *a vision to continuously grow into*.

> A Brahmin is not a Brahmin because he is born a Brahmin, but because his body is an arrow and his soul is a bow and with all his might he is aiming his soul at being Brahmin.
>
> *Herman Hesse,* Siddhartha

A brand essence is not a brand essence because you state it; a brand essence exists only to the extent your whole organization actively generates this essence.

Making money is why your company exists, but let's put that aside for this exercise. Why do customers give you money? Hannibal Lecter coached, "Read Marcus Aurelius. Of each particular thing ask: what is it in itself?"

For Corona, drinking their beer isn't about the flavor or getting a buzz as much as it is a statement of "this is play time."

Most people aren't buying the function of a product, but rather their associations with the brand or the feelings of the style—they're buying something beyond the function. You see, there's a function that a product or service fills, and then there's a bigger space with an emotional benefit. And *emotions are the key to loyalty*. Consistently promising and delivering on an emotion creates loyalty. You desire unreasonable customers, customers willing to pay more than average for a product and not to think about any other source for their satisfaction.

Consistency is the backbone of a longstanding trust. What follow in the next chapter are tools for consistency and continuity of messaging—"Legendary Branding."

Make a list of inconsistencies between your materials. What can be tighter? Are you using the same vocabulary throughout? Are there promises made in marketing that aren't reinforced in packaging? Tell your users what benefits they are enjoying. Your packaging and your product are your marketing for your next sale. Make them happy.

_____

_____

_____

_____

_____

_____

_____

_____

_____

7 | Legendary Branding

I've made up a few branding systems: Memetic Branding, Agricultural Branding, DNA Branding, and Legendary Branding. They're all structurally similar, they just use different models. Of these, Legendary Branding is consistently the easiest to understand. So I'm giving it to you here, but first let's review what we've covered so far.

I use PowerPoint slides here because PowerPoint is the medium of business, such that I'm more accustomed to writing about business in PowerPoint than I am in text. I use these PowerPoint slides in formal business presentations. Figure 7.1 starts with some of the basics we've learned about brands.

Since your brand is not your logo, I'm not overly concerned with minor inconsistencies in color or size. Should minor errors exist in your communications? No. I'm just saying that there are more important things with which you can concern yourself than minor differences or tiny flaws on marketing materials.

Figure 7.2, the second slide, gives more basics about brands and introduces the idea of a story or legend. Figure 7.3 then defines this concept to help you think about how this applies to brands.

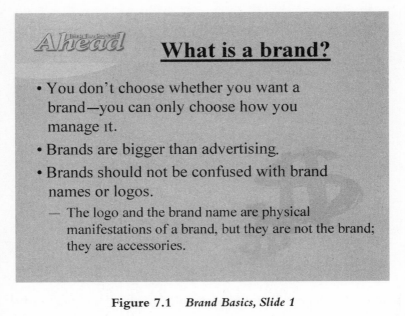

Figure 7.1   *Brand Basics, Slide 1*

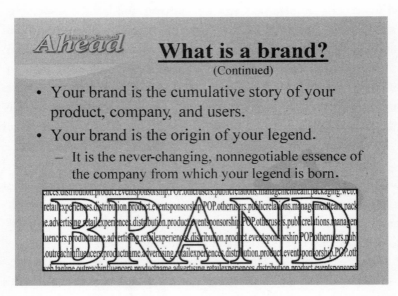

Figure 7.2   *Brand Basics, Slide 2*

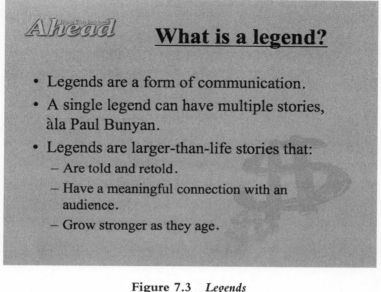

Figure 7.3 *Legends*

Brands *live in their stories.* Some of the stories are seeded by commercials and other communications like packaging, web sites, and answering machine messages. However, there are many, many stories about our products and services that we don't script. "Yesterday, when we ordered a Domino's Pizza . . ."—those kind of stories. Why is it people feel more compelled to share negative experiences? I don't know, but for the sake of your brand, please try and keep your customers happy. For my sake, I hope you find these ideas actionable and profitable.

Figure 7.4 expands the idea of legends and how they relate to your product. Let me highlight the second item: "Your customer is your story's hero. Your product or service is what facilitates their heroic activities." Sounds great—but these words are meaningless unless their application helps people make more money.

The greatest honor of writing a business book is having people I have never met take my words seriously and work through these ideas

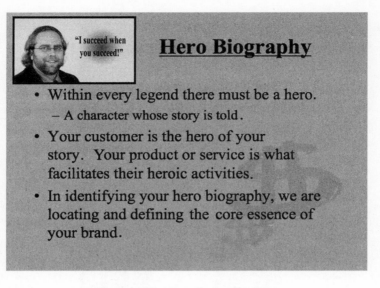

Figure 7.4 *Introducing the Hero*

for themselves. The greatest thrill is when they share how it has helped them. Joost van der Leij has profited from these ideas. When he wrote to me with suggestions for improvement I implemented as much as I could, knowing there were other readers with very similar perspectives. If I could make this material more usable to Joost, others would be more likely to replicate his success. Here's what Joost had to say:

> Before I received an advance copy of Ben Mack's *Think Two Products Ahead*, I was a "successful" direct response practitioner . . . Nice five figure income. Ever since I implemented these ideas from early January 2006 on, I have been adjusting my forecast upward. Originally I had planned for a 50% increase in sales in 2006, but today, March 1st, even *my most conservative forecasts mean doubling revenues in 2006.*
>
> - Google Click Through Rate jumped from 5.1% to 9.1%.
>
> - Subscriptions to my free newsletter increased from 100 to 150 per week to anything between 250 and 350 people each week.
>
> - Sales have gone up 206% month over month.

But going beyond the cold figures, I now have a much better understanding of my relationship with my clients, my communication with them and most important the reason why they choose to do business with me. I am happy to say that I now have found a process by which I am enabled to do the work I love most . . . for the rest of my life. *No more uncertainty about the future, for I am assured of more work than I can handle each and every day.*

Joost van der Leij, CEO, TIOUW.com BV
(For more information see http://www.tiouw.com/en/)

Who is your customer? Your hero. Your customer is the hero of your story—the person you are fighting to help be successful. Joost is my hero. The tools and techniques in this book facilitated his heroic business growth; Joost did the work and had the fortitude to follow through and implement these ideas.

Let's look at Clif Bar's hero, shown in Figure 7.5. Clif Bar is made by athletes for athletes. A Clif Bar user is somebody who has such a good time doing outdoor physical activities that they need extra energy in the form of an energy bar. But this person also enjoys great taste. The funky taste of a Power Bar just doesn't work for them, especially that chemical aftertaste.

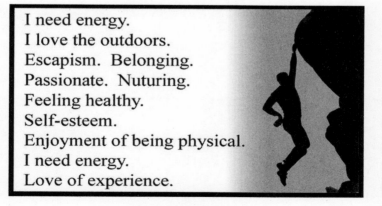

I need energy.
I love the outdoors.
Escapism. Belonging.
Passionate. Nuturing.
Feeling healthy.
Self-esteem.
Enjoyment of being physical.
I need energy.
Love of experience.

Figure 7.5 *Clif Bar's Hero*

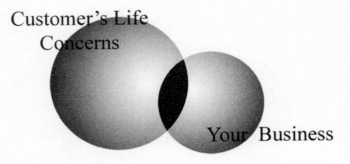

Talk about the stuff that overlaps, but which
stuff do you talk about?

Figure 7.6   *The Overlap between the Customer's Concerns and*
Your Business

Remember in Chapter 5 we mentioned the connection between your business and your customer's life concerns? Figure 7.6
emphasizes the need to be selective about what elements of that
overlap you highlight. Using the example of Clif Bars, Figure 7.7 lists
some of the positive overlaps that can be highlighted.

You want your customer to see themselves in your communications. As Figure 7.8 indicates, humans are tribal. We look for our
kind—the logos and flags that we see as "That's me."

The slides in Figures 7.9 and 7.10 outline more of the steps
involved in building this association between your product and

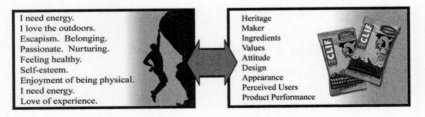

Figure 7.7   *Clif Bar Example of Positive Elements*

Figure 7.8   *Help Customers Identify with Your Product*

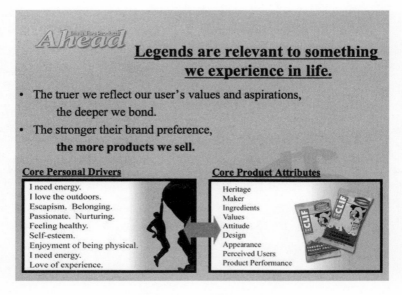

Figure 7.9   *Building Relevance*

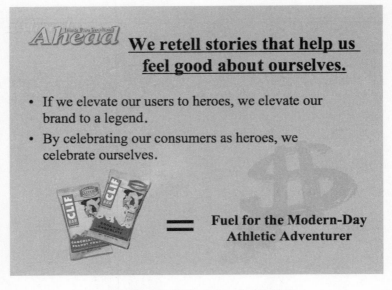

Figure 7.10   *Evolving the Legend*

your user's values, thereby enhancing the image of your product in their minds.

How do we use this information for consistent communications? Figure 7.11 names two messages we seek to convey.

Your Legend Platform communicates your brand essence in such a way that:

- Communications have emotional objectives. Advertising, packaging, and collateral have a unified vision to build.

- Teammates know what they are working toward. Employees have a tool that teaches and reinforces best practices by showing a big-picture vision of the consumer's experience.

Figure 7.12 shows Clif Bar's approach to creating its Legend Platform.

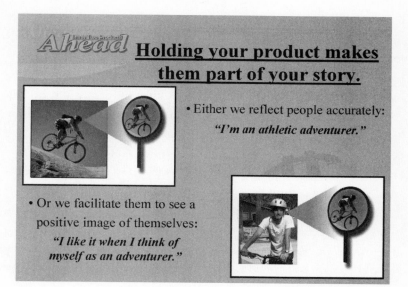

Figure 7.11 *Helping People See Themselves as Heroes*

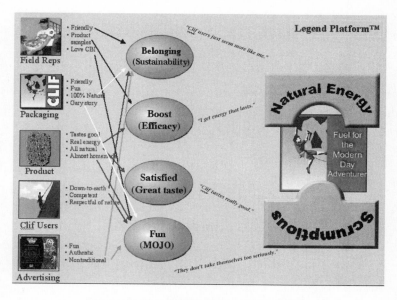

Figure 7.12 *Clif Bar's Legend Platform*

After working out this process, Clif Bar was more comfortable thinking of itself as standing for "Mojo" than "Fuel For The Modern Day Adventurer." That's fine. Its ads regularly show an athlete accomplishing something outrageously kooky (heroic) that requires extraordinary energy (fuel). That's Clif Bar Mojo. Other ads discuss the efficacy of their natural products and how good they taste. That's Clif Bar Mojo.

Clif Bar marketers have a great intuitive sense of what they are communicating because they are a community of their target audience. However, if you look at a broad portfolio of their communications you will likely find the ideas outlined here.

Branding is about sustainably making money—and making money from existing clients is paramount. Luna Bar was a great idea and proved to be extraordinarily profitable, but it wasn't an athletic bar and it wasn't designed for all Clif Bar eaters. Why confuse your existing user base? So they named this new bar Luna Bar. Well done, Clif Bar. While I worked on this account, what cracked me up was the e-mails they received asking if a guy eating a Luna Bar would grow breasts. The answer is no, go ahead. These bars are tasty and good for you, nothing bad for guys in them—you just don't need the folic acid or vitamin K.

I hold that the brilliance behind Luna Bar is often underrecognized. The bars have frosting on only one side—just a little bit of indulgence, a perfect design for a women's product. If you think I'm being sexist with that statement, you're right. Get over it. I'm here to help you make money.

Look at the next example of a Legend Platform, this one created for GameWorks' original store in Seattle, Washington. (See Figure 7.13.) As a side note, GameWorks no longer uses this platform, but GW evolved from this. GameWorks paid $60,000 to Fattal & Collins for this diagram in 1997. (I was the brand strategist working with Eric Hirschberg and Mike Sheldon before that team headed up Deutsch LA, where I later joined them. Deutsch LA won "Ad Agency of the Year" twice while the three of us worked together.

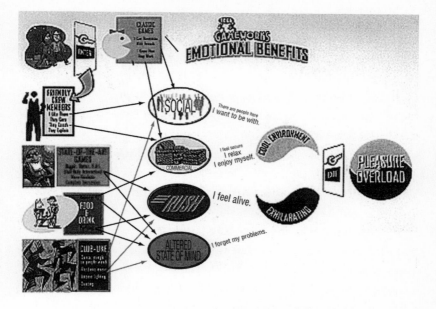

Figure 7.13 *GameWorks' Legend Platform*

However, I was under the tutelage of Jeffrey Blish, who taught me how to be an ad guy. Hirschberg is a genius. I was lucky to be there.)

From this GameWorks' Legend Platform, we can see that Game-Works was standing for "Pleasure Overload." It had the most extreme games and deliciously seasoned fries and decadent drinks. If it had continued down this path, GameWorks would look very different today. Instead, it went down a more mass and family friendly direction, which redefined the target audience.

Early on, this sheet was used to communicate the GameWorks culture to everyone from in-store employees to architects. If something in or about GameWorks was *not* communicating or reinforcing a sense of being social or comfortable, or generating an adrenaline rush or an altered state of mind, it wasn't GameWorks. The goal was for somebody leaving GameWorks to feel satiated.

Here's a minor technicality: Some marketers want their brand essence to be a promise, like "pleasure overload," while others want their brand essence to be a benefit, like feeling satiated. I don't see a substantive difference between thinking of your brand essence as your primal benefit or your big promise. The key is putting your customer first in terms of their experience.

The two previous examples of a Legend Platform are well art-directed. I don't have these skills and, frankly, they aren't necessary for communicating to yourself or a small team. I don't want you to be stopped by a lack of graphic design capabilities. The pictures aren't what makes this work. What makes these platforms useful is the construction and how it illustrates the relationship between your attributes, your customer benefits, and your brand essence or brand promise. However, some visual thinkers find that drawing the pictures is part of how they work through the ideas. My point is that creating a Legend Platform is basically filling out a worksheet. The ideas and their interconnectedness are more important right now than how pretty it looks. If you work at a big company and want to share it with executives, hire an art director. Instead of art directing, you can fill out this form—but not yet.

First, let's look at a familiar example: Marlboro. (*Huge* caveat here: I've never worked on a tobacco product, let alone Marlboro.) I made up the diagram in Figure 7.14 as if I were Marlboro's brand manager. I'm not claiming any knowledge of the marketing of Marlboro other than what I can see in the marketplace and what Jay Levinson explained to me when I was interviewing him for the video *The Pitch, Poker and The Public*, edited and directed by Chris Zubryd.

If I were Marlboro's brand manager, I would know their brand essence. Since I don't, I'll pretend Marlboro's Essence is "Strength and Independence." If I were the brand manager, I'd look at every communication and ask: "Does _____ reinforce a sense of strength and independence?"

Please notice, I'm not asking if the communication reinforces a sense of cowboy. I don't think Marlboro salesmen should wear west-

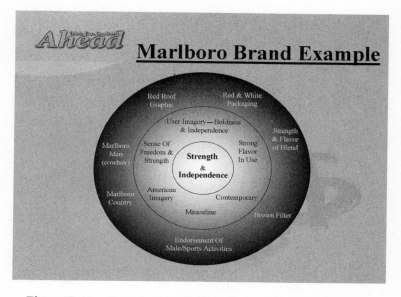

Figure 7.14   *Hypothetical Marlboro Legend Platform Worksheet*

ern apparel and cowboy boots. Marlboro isn't selling "cowboy"—they're selling "Strength and Independence." Cowboy is one of their tools standing for strength and independence. If Marlboro was intending to stand for cowboy then they wouldn't sponsor Nascar or other non–equestrian sporting events.

Now it's your turn. Using the diagram shown in Figure 7.15, start with the outer ring and fill in the attributes by writing in what a consumer might see, hear, and touch in terms of your product. (See Appendix C for another approach to constructing an entrepreneur's Legend Platform.)

Next, what are the benefits that happen through these experiences? Write down more than you can use. Be bold. Make your lists of attributes and use the attributes to come up with your benefits. After you have exhausted these lists, turn the page and learn what to do next in Chapter 8. However, please don't move on until you've made these lists.

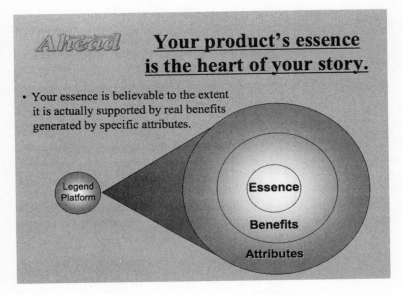

Figure 7.15 *The Legend Platform Includes Attributes, Benefits, and Essence*

EXERCISE 7

1. You saw the exercise described previously, right? Take a stab at these lists. Write down the benefits and attributes for your products and services.

_____

_____

_____

_____

_____

_____

2. As you read the rest of this book, carve out your own exercises and disregard what you don't find a profitable use of your time.

_____

_____

_____

_____

_____

_____

Important note: Authenticity is important. If you are selling Elvis memorabilia and you don't love Elvis, you won't sell as much as somebody who authentically loves Elvis. So if you don't share your target's love and passion, I suggest hiring people who do. Laws prohibit marketers from making many boldfaced lies. Human intuition takes care of some of the rest. People can smell authenticity. Keep it real.

8

Extracting a
Brand Essence

Before we discuss what to do with your lists, I'd like to talk you through how I like to approach this kind of assignment with consumer research to help guide me in extracting a brand essence.

Research . . . I find loyal and happy patrons and I ask them the most open-ended question I can: "When you think of GameWorks, what comes to mind?" Figure 8.1 shows the basic framework of the questioning process. I draw a circle and place the vital demographics of my participant in this circle. I write down each attribute they mention about GameWorks. I avoid questions that allow them to answer yes or no. When they are running out of steam, I ask, "What else can you think of?"

Then I ask about a specific attribute. "You mentioned classic games. What do classic games bring to mind? . . . Uh-huh. What else? . . . Uh-huh. What's that like?" I'm listening for emotional benefits around which I later draw a star. Figure 8.2 contains some actual field notes from some of the 42 interviews I conducted (my penmanship isn't great).

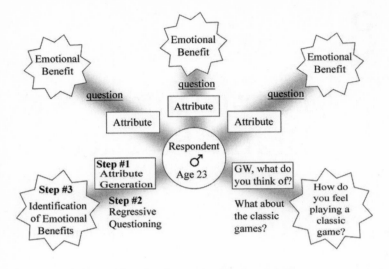

Figure 8.1   *Framework for Research Questions*

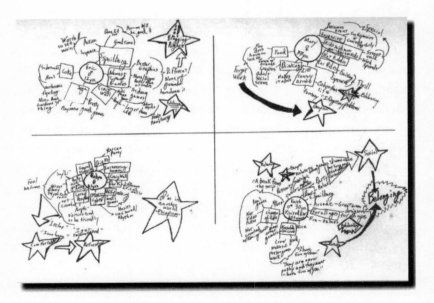

Figure 8.2   *Field Notes from Author's Interviews*

I then analyze the data. I start by looking at the emotional benefits. Many times there will be several similar emotional benefits; part of my job is clustering these emotions and choosing an appropriate label. Next, I tabulate the number of mentions for each attribute, again clustering similar items as required. Then I try sketching out this information, as demonstrated in Figure 8.3.

Do you see what I did there? I connected physical attributes to emotional benefits. I looked at what emotional benefits regularly emerged from what attributes and began to fill in common quotes that supported these connections.

This draft is reviewed by management and adjusted accordingly. Management buy-in is critical—you don't have a brand vision if you are the only person that can see it. The emotional benefits are reviewed and tweaked as necessary. Together, as a group, we decide on the overarching emotional benefit—also known as a brand promise. Figure 8.4 shows the completed diagram.

However, even big-budget clients don't want to budget money for consumer research to develop communications. This astounds me. How can a company spend $20,000,000 on advertising but refuse to

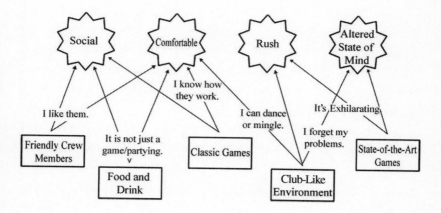

Figure 8.3 *Matching Attributes and Benefits*

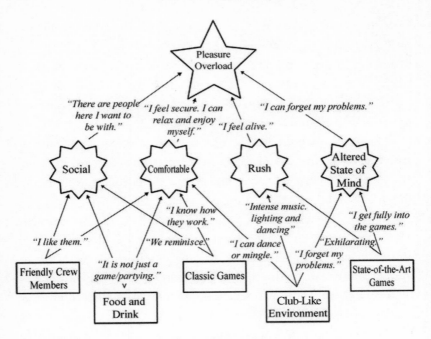

Figure 8.4   *Completed Brand Essence Analysis*

spend $30,000 to understand the emotional impact of their product or service? I must suck at adequately explaining the benefits of these learnings. However, they're often willing to spend money on testing communications. Let me ask you this: How do we know what we want to test? I respect industry norms, but unusual tactics offer your best chance of radical success, and industry norms often have little to do with strange strategies.

Without this kind of consumer research, I do what you did: I make lists of attributes and I speculate on the associated consumer benefits. A good buddy of mine named Rich Goidel made a board game called Sea Rats that celebrates being a pirate. Below is an initial list I made of attributes and benefits, along with my amped-up version.

Sea Rats Attributes	Sea Rats Benefits	Sea Rats Amped Benefits
Web site	Strategy	Swagger
Board	Fun	Pillaging
Instructions	Pirate speak	Role-playing
Play with friends	Discovery	Adventurous
Game pieces	Winning	Conquering
Die	Drinking (optional)	Carousing
Treasure	Social	Becoming mates
Real ports		Immersive
E-mail updates		Masquerading
Ships		Satiating
Game play		

There's a fine line between amped emotions and puffery or hype. Nobody likes vacuous hype, but when people get into this game, they really get into acting like a pirate. The allure of Sea Rats isn't about the board game, but an excuse to act like a pirate. I look at the list of amped benefits and I ask myself, "What is this really?" Or, as Marcus Aurelius asked, "What is it in itself?" Sea Rats gives players pirate biographies and puts players into pirate scenarios, set in historic pirate ports, described in pirate terminology. Playing Sea Rats facilitates being a pirate.

Sea Rats's appeal is not about the game play, but about what people do while they're playing the game. Sea Rats is a catalyst to a pirate state of mind. Sea Rats is a pirate portal—by playing the game you create a realm of pirates and bounty and booty and carousing. We landed on "Pirate Lore" as our brand essence. (See Figure 8.5.)

How is this useful? On a single page is a schematic of the tones and goals of Rich's product and communications. Rich re-engineered the game to be less complicated and focus more on authentic pirate trivia, reinforcing the essence of "Pirate Lore." All of the game's collateral is chock-full of pirate terms and real pirate names and places, steeped in pirate heritage that is brought to the forefront by the play of

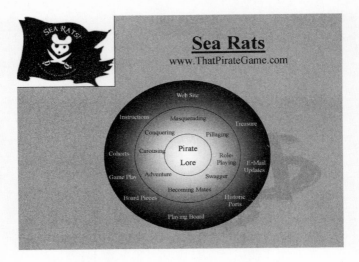

Figure 8.5   *Elements of Sea Rats' Brand Essence*

the game. Players are encouraged to bring their pirate gear. Just check out his web site to see what I mean: www.ThatPirateGame.com. (Note: Rich is still revising this site.)

1. Create your own exercises based on the material discussed in this chapter.

_____

_____

2. Find a way to speak with happy and loyal customers of your competitor(s) and ask them why they are so happy. Don't sell them on yourself—research participants can smell that agenda. Your mission in this conversation is to understand what makes your competitor's loyal customers so loyal.

9

The Kama Sutra of Marketing: Five Basic Positions

How many ways can you cook an egg? I want you to stop reading and make a list of how many ways you can think of to cook an egg. I'm not talking about as an ingredient, I'm talking about hard-boiled, fried . . . How many other ways can you list? Go on—make your list.

Thank you for making your list. It will make what I'm about to discuss more impactful, more valuable to you. I can see three ways to cook an egg: fried, scrambled, and boiled. Yes, there is also "over easy"—but isn't that just fried and flipped over while the yolk is still runny? There's an omelet, but that's just scrambled and then flipped over on itself. Okay, poached is different from hard-boiled or soft-boiled. But you see my point. The level of complexity in classification is up to you. I'm going to talk about five general types of positionings, but you can make up as many as you want.

How many folds are in a traditional chef's hat? There are 103. Why? Because there are 103 ways to cook an egg, not as an ingredient, but 103 ways to cook a single egg. That's great. I've talked to several chefs about this and they say that there are basically 15 to 23 ways to cook an egg and that the rest are simply degrees of cooking. My point here is that many times, less is more. You know this.

The taxonomy I gave you for cooking an egg—fried, scrambled, or boiled—is by no means exhaustive; many would argue the number should be at least five or seven. I agree that three ways of cooking an egg is too limited to be useful. Where do you classify a poached egg?

Similarly, I'm going to give you a taxonomy of positionings, 5 basic positionings, that could be expanded to 7, or 9, or 103. For company positionings, I find this set of 5 useful:

1. What you offer.

2. What you do.

3. How you do it.

4. Who you are.

5. Why you do it.

Discussing positioning without products is like playing poker without cards, it can be done, but it becomes a different game.

Let's discuss wireless communications. I'm creating Table 9.1 in January 2006, so this isn't revealing privileged information from when I was senior vice president and brand strategy director at BBDO, working on Cingular.

It can be easily argued that Verizon belongs in the "Who You

Table 9.1   Example of Five Basic Positionings

What You Offer (Products/ Services)	What You Have (Infrastructure)	How You Do It (Process)	Who You Are (Core Value)	Why You Do It (Mission/Purpose)
MetroPCS is a low-price service offering: "Permission to speak freely." Sprint/Nextel help you "work."	Verizon touts "We never stop working for you" and claims to have the most reliable network.	Sprint/Nextel appear to be heading in this direction by touting a different type of network.	Cingular touts excellence with "Raising the bar" but its ads are all about products and services without a quality claim.	MetroPCS could take on this space: "Because wireless shouldn't be so expensive."

Are" bucket. Fine, try that out. There are multiple right answers to this game. The purpose is to have a structure that allows you to see possibilities and begin to define the lay of the land. This is work that your customers and prospective customers won't see—that's why this work is often thought of as irrelevant and complicated. Yet you are composing the framework that will make your company's story distinctive and attractive in the marketplace.

One of these positions is inherently stronger than the rest: mission. If you can make your product feel like it is a mission, a worthy cause, you have energy! However, there are few things as distasteful as a phony mission that takes itself too seriously. A rare exception is a Southern California ski resort that gives excuses for missing work and not paying rent: "Because you gotta ski!" Then again, that mission is real to the ardent skier who needs to ski. Just be careful, because a fake mission will ring false and only your prices will attract customers.

In different categories and different times, various positions may be stronger. So what's the value? The value is that this gives you a framework to think of your company's offering. These divisions are not mutually exclusive nor completely exhaustive, but it gives you a framework to reconsider what your company or product really offers.

In 1996 I worked on a consumer research study for Sunkist when they were testing a repositioning for their Fruit Roll Ups. They had been sold in the candy aisle and had positioned themselves as a healthy snack. An ingenious brand manager said that they were made from 100 percent fruit and should therefore be sold in the produce department. He was trying on different possibilities, shown in Table 9.2.

Sunkist Fruit Roll Ups were surrounded by a bunch of competitive roll-up snacks and his product looked just like other roll-ups that were loaded with sugar. Consumer research showed that

Table 9.2 Possible Repositionings for Fruit Roll Ups

What You Offer (Products/ Services)	What You Have (Infrastructure)	How You Do It (Process)	Who You Are (Core Value)	Why You Do It (Mission/Purpose)
Healthy snack	100% fruit	No sugar added	Natural	Healthier folks

this new positioning made sense to consumers—the new placement in Ralphs grocery stores in Southern California had three times the sales of the previous location. Nowadays you can find all sorts of crap in the produce section. So it goes—the landscape keeps changing.

Try this for your own company or for one of your products. Fill-in each bucket for your company or for a specific product, or maybe you have two or three ideas for each bucket—great! Write them down in the blanks provided here.

What You Offer (Products/ Services)	What You Have (Infrastructure)	How You Do It (Process)	Who You Are (Core Value)	Why You Do It (Mission/Purpose)
_____	_____	_____	_____	_____
_____	_____	_____	_____	_____
_____	_____	_____	_____	_____

Now think about your competition. Use the next form to write down who's saying what.

What You Offer (Products/ Services)	What You Have (Infrastructure)	How You Do It (Process)	Who You Are (Core Value)	Why You Do It (Mission/Purpose)
_____	_____	_____	_____	_____
_____	_____	_____	_____	_____
_____	_____	_____	_____	_____

Now look and see if there are buckets that are empty. Maybe these buckets are empty because it just hasn't worked for your product. Maybe it's fruitless trying to go down this path. Then again, maybe this is an untapped opportunity.

How you present your company or product affects a customer's experience and expectation. I'm not giving you answers—I'm offering you different ways to revisit familiar material that might spark new ideas, what in consumer research is referred to as an insight.

These five basic positions are *not* positioning statements. These positions are considerations for what you emphasize in your framing. They are guidelines and are not mutually exclusive. In fact, you could get fancy and use all five positionings in one communication. However, I suggest that you choose one overarching, primary positioning and use it consistently. The subordinate positionings can be framed as reasons to believe the overarching positioning.

The more experience you get, the easier it will be to break more guidelines with success. As you start out, keep it simple and clear by simply choosing one positioning.

The next chapter on framing is critical. I show you how I play with ideas. *Critical* has four primary meanings:

1. Expressing adverse or disapproving comments.

2. Expressing analysis of the merits.

3. Having the potential to be disastrous.

4. Having crucial importance.

I primarily mean that fourth definition, "having crucial importance." However, all four definitions will be appropriate at different times.

1. I express disapproving comments of an ill-named product.

2. I discuss the process of analysis of the merits of ideas and connections.

3. I use politics as an example of framing that might be disastrous to my sales.

4. Framing has crucial importance.

While reading this book, your understanding of *critical* is dependent on how I use the word; the context I give the word shades its meaning.

EXERCISE 9

1. Review the lists you created in the previous two chapters for possible positionings. How might your communications, packaging, and products change if you fully embraced that positioning as a core focus of your company?

_____

_____

_____

_____

2. Go bolder. Try amping up each list. Is passion emerging? Dwell on the positioning that feels passionate and then execute on whatever appears most profitable.

_____

_____

_____

_____

_____

3. Test your executions. Whenever possible, use split tests to ascertain which of two ideas is more profitable. In a split test you run two communications at the same time and see which one is more profitable. Is there anything you can start testing today? Do you have a newsletter with some sort of call to action? The next time you send your newsletter, can you print two different calls to action and see which one pulls more?

10 | Framing to the Right Target Audience

Framing is about what you bring to the forefront of your customer's mind. The positioning we discussed in Chapter 9 is a form of framing.

Look at the cube in Figure 10.1. You can see the darker side of this cube as either the closest side to you or the backside. (If you can't see both right away, just give it a minute.)

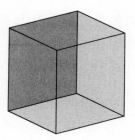

Figure 10.1   *An Exercise in Framing*

89

Table 10.1   **Five Positionings for Tax Structure**

What You Offer (Product/Service)	What You Have (Infrastructure)	How You Do It (Process)	Who You Are (Core Value)	Why You Do It (Mission/Purpose)
Regressive tax	Simple tax	Flat tax	Pro-business	Fair tax

Powerful examples of framing are commonplace in politics. You've heard some politicians rant about the need for the "fair tax." Did you know that this same tax structure has been called the "flat tax" and what traditional economists would call a "regressive tax"? Which of these names feels most compelling? Fairness, right? Take a look at it relative to the five positionings introduced in the previous chapter (see Table 10.1).

It is difficult to argue against a fair tax! Labels shape our feelings and sentiments regardless of what the content really is. It is difficult to vote against a Patriot Act. What senator wants to be seen as unpatriotic? (Note: Some readers may mistakenly assume I'm a Democrat because I use examples provided by the dominant political party. I'm neither a Democrat nor a Republican. I don't want to get into politics here. I fondly remember the days when calling a dirty politician "a liar and a crook" was not labeled as subversive but patriotic and brave. I've done consumer research for Scientology, but I'm not a Scientologist. I'm a profiteer.)

Framing is about packaging ideas to make them more compelling to *your target audience*. Here's a real-life example: In 1998 two search engines framed their services in very different ways. Which of these is more compelling?

1. "A better way to search."

2. "Find what you're looking for."

Why do you use a search engine? For the joy of searching? No! Your goal is to *find*. Focusing on the consumer benefit is far more compelling than describing functionality. Yahoo! used "Find what you're looking for." Google touted "A better way to search." For several years more people used Yahoo! than Google. Once again, Carville and Begala were right:

> Military strategists know that most battles are won before the first shot is fired—by the side that determines where, when and how an engagement is fought. . . . Political professionals call the act of defining the terrain of engagement "framing the debate."
>
> *James Carville and Paul Begala,* Buck Up, Suck Up
> *(New York: Simon & Schuster, 2003)*

This battle was won at the word *find*. However, a battle is not the war. Google is winning on *many* fronts. In 1998, Web surfers didn't know much about search engines. "A better way to search" was appealing to those who were Web-savvy. Google is hugely successful, and I'm *not* saying that what Google said wasn't optimal. I'm just saying it didn't have the mass appeal of what Yahoo! was saying. Google may not have been going for mass—they may have been seeking to more deeply entrench with investors and VCs. Different target audiences will appreciate different messages. I didn't work on either of these accounts, so I don't know what their intentions were. My qualm with most case studies is that they are either exercises in speculation written by people who weren't there or self-serving propaganda that makes all the participants appear as brilliant.

I wrote the American Marketing Association's Effie application for Yomega Yo Yos. We won. You think I was more concerned with writing a comprehensively accurate application or a more selective one that made us look good? You're not actually pondering the previous question, are you? Of course I wrote the application to make all of our efforts look intentional and effective. I'm good, but if I were that intentionally effective I wouldn't be writing this book. There would be reporters lined up to interview me about how idea propagation really works. I'd be called the Edward Bernays of the twenty-first century. Who is Edward Bernays? He's the man who popularized smoking among women; the work of his uncle, Sigmund Freud; the overthrow of several governments for the benefit of the United Fruit Company; and the idea that every kid should learn to play the piano. For more on Edward Bernays, please see www.ThinkTwoProductsAhead.com/Bernays. Thank you.

Look, few case studies are written about failed projects that you've never heard of by the folks that helped create the flop. Along these lines, I doubt I'll write a case study on my championing Baskin-Robbins' failed Warm Cookie Sundae, but in my speaking engagements I use that story to teach a lesson. Nevertheless, I'm encouraging you not to take my word, or anybody else's word, as gospel.

Develop your own guidelines for success. Test and refine. Be skeptical of what you cannot prove. Marketing has an agenda but it is often invisible to outsiders. The most important business skill to develop is your ability to ascertain what is making you money and how to make more. Trust your success, not what I or any expert tells you. I might have done something lucky once, but if you can't replicate it, my success should be called entertainment.

At multiple big agencies, on several occasions, I have worked on crafting ads that ran in mass publications but were *not* targeting consumers. These ads looked like consumer ads, but they were really targeted to buyers at major retailers, to demonstrate that we listened to them. These buyers then ordered more of our product and the product sold better with premium exposure to customers on the retailers' shelves. This is part of why modeling your tactics on high-visibility, nationally marketed products is dangerous: Unless you worked on the project, you often don't know the real objectives.

Please don't talk to me about how scholastic journals are objective and an objective source of learning. Some of my best friends are professors. I wish my professor friends could focus on teaching and actual research. However, most high-paying professorships have a publish-or-perish condition of employment. Professors can dig and prod, but they can't accurately report intent of marketing initiatives. Successful projects have extended families and failures appear to be orphans. I can prove to you that academic subjects aren't objective.

How come I can't find a single class on marketing pornography in any American business school? A multibillion-dollar-a-year category appears grossly understudied and untaught by American universities, except that—well, it's porn. Being perceived as endorsing pornography endangers grants and endowments that may otherwise come to a university.

Why am I discussing pornography? Remember what it felt like when I said, "That's bunk!" in Chapter 2? Had I written "bullsh★t," many readers would have disregarded this whole manual. Why am I using the word now? Because I figure we know each other well enough now that I can get away with using a synonym for crap. I'm sorry if I've offended you. Sincerely, I'm sorry, because I want your money, and you are here because you want my skills to help you make more money. Sometimes I'm gruff. I'm sorry, but I like writing the way I talk and I tend to call stuff the way I see it. This may raise your hackles. This is good. This means I'm charging neurons that haven't been charged recently. If you keep doing what you have been doing you will get what you've always gotten, only less, because the competition is getting steeper. You want *more*.

Do you want to make *more* money or do you want to be comforted? Answer this honestly, please. I've been studying Direct Response marketing for the past year. I find more smarts in these independent folks than I have found in big agencies. The average successful DR practitioner is better read and more data savvy than 99 percent of the folks I've met in traditional agencies. However, I find remarkably little coverage of Direct Response marketing in business schools. These are masters of effectiveness. Carl Rove started in Direct Response marketing. It's difficult to argue with effectiveness. I admire and study effective persuasion. I don't always agree with how this technology is used.

KiiC

I don't mean to burn bridges, but I do. I owe an apology to the brand manager on KiiC, the defunct product name for Cingular's prepaid cell phones, a doomed product that was finally put out of its misery with the merger with AT&T Wireless. GO Phone is far better. Perhaps you just said, "KiiC, like 'keep in contact,' but there's an extra 'i.'"

Dear KiiC Brand Manager,

I'm sorry I hurt your feelings when I worked at BBDO. And I'm sorry if I'm hurting your feelings now, but *your baby was ugly*. If you're a mom, I'm not talking about the featherless-biped you call your child, I'm talking about KiiC. Stupid name against your larger target.

Yes, this name makes sense against 14-year-olds looking to get a phone without having to sign a contract. But the vast majority of people buying a prepaid phone are credit-challenged adults, not 14-year-olds.

Credit-challenged folks don't like to be reminded that they have bad credit. They respond to respect. They don't want to feel derogated. If 13 percent of the 18-plus-year-old customers wanting to buy a phone fail the credit screen, which phone is easier to sell them next? A KiiC phone or a GO phone.

Now, I handled this poorly. I shouldn't have said in an aghast voice, "Why would we name it *that*?" I'm sorry. That just came out of my mouth. But seriously . . . how the *fornication* can you think like that? I'm seriously curious how this made sense to you.

With regret,

Ben

Warning: Don't do drugs and fall in love with what you create. If you insist on writing drunk, then at least edit sober—and test your ideas with real customers.

If you want to hire me to justify your failures I can do that, but I have a hard time being told I'm being hired to help somebody make money only to learn that that's not the objective. I can help you get what you want; however, the job is easier when you know what you want and can articulate these objectives in specific, measurable results.

Marketing is about influencing people, being a social engineer. I happen to specialize in marketing with direct profit agendas, but I am most proud of work I did at TG Madison for the American Cancer Society. The specific, measurable result we sought was unreasonable: to get substantively more men age 50 and older to get a colonoscopy, an uncomfortable procedure where a patient doesn't eat for 12 hours and then has a scope stuck up his ass to assess whether he might have cancer.

We had about a $10 million budget. Generally, you can't do squat on a national level with a $10 million advertising budget. We spent only $6 million advertising to the general population of men. We spent $4 million advertising to doctors explaining to them what we were telling *their* patients.

We got great results. Why? Because we leveraged the doctors' egos. Doctors need to be experts. When we told the doctors that we were educating their patients, they absorbed our message and began encouraging their patients to get a colonoscopy. This may appear to be a strange strategy. It would have been very difficult to ascertain our objectives from the outside. Furthermore, the American Cancer Society (ACS) would never allow TG Madison to brag about this strategy in public because this strategy may strain the relationship between ACS and doctor associations.

Before you decide on an optimal framing, you must make sure you are addressing your optimal target. Your optimal target will have many triggers to take action. In what ways might you best compel your optimal target?

EXERCISE 10

Who is most important to reaching your sales goals? This is your real target. What are the real politics? How can you work the politics in your favor?

_____

_____

_____

_____

_____

11

Structured Creativity: Framing Tools

Most jazz musicians are also really good at playing scales. Most abstract expressionist painters are really good at figure drawings. In Chapter 12 I discuss more free-form ideating, generating ideas like Orville Redenbacher popped popcorn. But for now, let's look at some structured tools.

I learned commercial idea manipulation from focus group moderators. It is amazing how resistant business folks can be to doing exercises themselves that they find value in watching consumers do. If you want to work with me, I might make you uncomfortable at times—but I'll probably help you make more money. What I'm giving you in this manual is what I do before I facilitate a "Brand Strategy Offsite" for companies. You can do these exercises yourself, or you can just keep reading and think that reading about these exercises will help you make money.

I want you to get some index cards and write the names of your competitors on the cards. The example I'm going to use is Airlines.

At WongDoody I worked on Alaska Airlines through the 9/11 repositioning—but that's a story for another forum.

As in Figure 11.1, write down the names of all your competitors on index cards or on blank pages torn into quarters. This doesn't need to be neat and tidy—ripping up paper will work for this exercise. Just do the work, please. Thank you.

Now arrange them. How? It doesn't matter. Just arrange them; simple groupings can be big and small companies. Figure 11.2 shows a set of cards divided into big and small airlines.

You can just mess them around and look for connections. Returning for a moment to the cube we looked at in Chapter 10 (see Figure 11.3), we're looking for ways of seeing the landscape that we haven't noticed before.

Dividing them up into big and small isn't likely to produce insights. What's an insight? Something that makes you go "Aha!" or

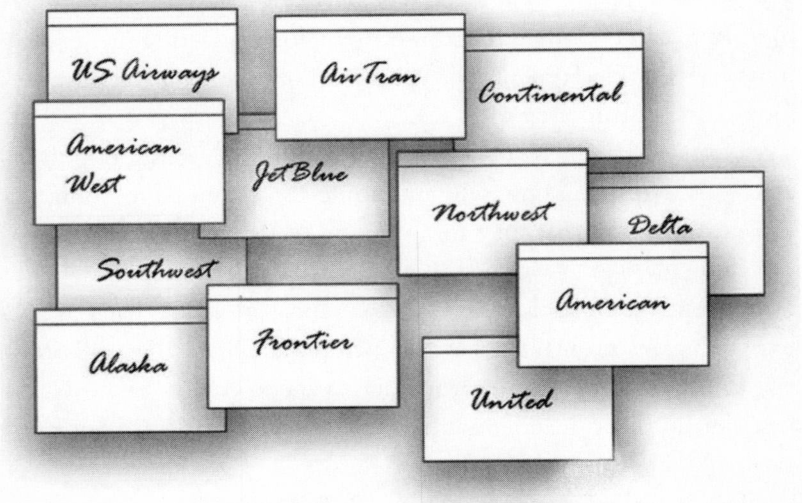

Figure 11.1 *Writing Names on Cards*

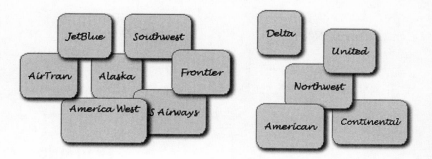

Figure 11.2   *Arranging the Cards in Groups*

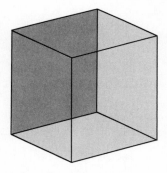

Figure 11.3   *Try Seeing Things in More than One Way*

"Hmm . . . ," a perspective that allows you to see your subject in a way you have never looked at it before.

Figure 11.4 offers another simple organization: by general positioning. The labels I've thrown in are very basic.

Now, I might change the labels on each group. For example, "style" isn't a very clear description of that small group. If a new label changes the way I see the groups, I might change the groups around. I take notes on what I see. I find notes help me sort the information later.

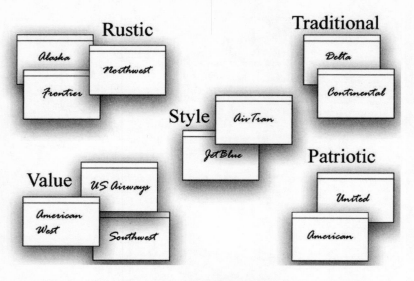

Figure 11.4 *Organizing the Cards by General Positioning*

This is part of the prep work I do before I lead a Brand Strategy Offsite for companies. At J. Walter Thompson we called it a "Day 1." Working with OMD it was called "Checkmate" (a very comprehensive and accessible planning system), and other brand agencies have different names for their systems.

Many times I would do exercises like this with participants in focus groups, and then in the Brand Strategy Offsite I would present these findings. Since you're reading this book, I imagine you are doing this for your own company. So you are doing this for real—you are playing with money that is real to you. I love that. I can get frustrated working with corporate heads who are playing with money that isn't real to them, because they just want to have fun.

I imagine you are actually working through these exercises—I hope I'm correct. Now take your brand card and randomly pick up

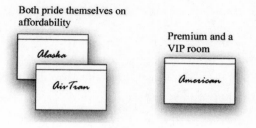

Figure 11.5   *Naming Similarities and Differences*

two others. Put two of these cards together and one to the side, as shown in Figure 11.5. Describe how the two companies you put together are similar to each other and how the third is different from them.

This work can seem tedious. It's not like there is one formula that allows you to get a great positioning. If that were the case, a computer program would be the best marketer. Hell, that might happen. Computers can now consistently beat humans at many things. Cool stuff on that, but again that's not what we're here to talk about. Figure 11.6 gives another example of grouping similarities and differences.

Get a customer to tell you their perceptions. Doing this with customers will yield different responses than doing this exercise with

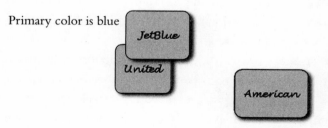

Figure 11.6   *Another Example of Similarity and Difference*

a corporate employee or executive. With customers you want to talk to at least two groups:

1. Loyals—those who love your product and service and are sticking with it. Learn what they love about your brand and why they are excited.

2. Your core prospects—those who you are hoping will become loyalists but haven't yet.

Learning what your missed prospects see is often fascinating, but most company owners or brand managers can't have this conversation with a prospect because they start arguing with the participant. Perceptions aren't wrong—perceptions are merely perceptions. A belief might be wrong, and that can create in prospects a perception that cost you money. It is fabulously helpful to discover how they came to this belief.

This chapter might be perceived as esoteric by some readers. Some readers may be put off by the word *esoteric*, because they don't know that it means that the subject matter is difficult and likely to be understood by just a few. I'm okay with this. Framing your product from scratch takes work—mental work—and *play*.

Play with your cards for 10 minutes, taking notes on what you find. Then I want you to take a 10-minute recess.

I'm serious—stop doing this for 10 minutes. Thank you.

Okay, recess is over. Back to framing: Framing can be as much about what you don't say as it can be about what you do say. For some folks one word can kill a relationship—so why use them? My editor wanted me to take the "Bullsh★t" paragraph out because he thought it might hinder sales. I successfully argued that stretching your mind is part of what is required for working on framing. More traditional thinking is coming—but have you noticed how this chapter jumps around a lot? This is intentional. New stimulus sparks ideas.

Figure 11.7 *Banana Exercise*

Try this just for kicks: Look at the picture of a banana in Figure 11.7. Then list the attributes of a banana. Here's my list:

- Curved
- Comes in bunches
- Soft interior
- Sliceable
- Yellow
- Peelable

Now think about your product or company. If your product adopted one of these attributes, how could it be different? Go through each attribute and answer that same question.

Your mind can do marvelous maneuvers. For example, you can read the following paragraph, something that's been circulating around the Internet for a while:

It hradly mttaers in waht oredr the ltteers are in a wrod. The olny rlaely iprmoatnt tihng is taht the frist and lsat ltteer be in the rghit pclae. The

rset can be a taotl mses and you can sitll raed it wouthit too mnay por-
belms. Tihs is bcuseae the huamn mnid deos not raed ervey lteter by
istlef, but the wrod as a wlohe. Amzanig. I awlyas tghuhot slpeling was
oevr rtaed!

Back to linear thinking. Most companies have brand guidelines,
what they will and won't say to customers. Simply saying that you
won't use profanity is barely a beginning.

Nordstrom is concerned that people refer to the company as
"Nordstroms." So, one of their brand guidelines is that communications never use the possessive: Nordstrom's. Thus they might an-
nounce that there is "an Annual Shirt Sale at Nordstrom," but never
"Nordstrom's Annual Shirt Sale." Nordstrom also doesn't sell lingerie—it sells "discreet apparel," among many other synonyms.

Cingular has a little logo/icon that jumps around and says words
and phrases via a cute thought bubble. Part of my job was to rewrite
the guidelines for this icon. Originally, the brand guidelines suggested
that the icon could never bend or have a fluid movement, but Rich
Wakefield pointed out that when Cingular is a sponsor of Special
Olympics this felt wrong. Rich saw we could be misconstrued as
making fun of these Olympiads. So we broke that rule for those spots.

We went several steps further in defining the logo's character. We
made a list of two positive attributes that—wait, let me have you do
this before I tell you what we did. Make a list of 10 positive words.
Then go back down the list and write a similar word, a synonym in
the next column. Both lists should only be positive words.

We did this exercise for Cingular's icon. Actually we had a list of
about 400 paired attributes and chose either 12 or 14 for our final
list. Then we chose only one word from each pair of attributes. The
icon character was then defined as more "approachable" than "socia-
ble," among many other distinctions.

Why get this specific? Each of these distinctions is part of your
framing. Using consistent language helps build a stable idea in your
customer's mind. Think of people you know. If somebody has mood

1.	
2.	
3.	
4.	
5.	
6.	
7.	
8.	
9.	
10.	

swings, do you feel settled around them? Mood swings can be disorienting. Using different verbiage in your communications feels like mood swings to a reader.

This is often where branding gets a bad name. Consistency is important. The exact hue of the color of your logo is less important. It looks unprofessional to use five different fonts on a page. Where do you draw the line? I don't have an answer for you.

Repetition breeds familiarity. Repetition can create meaning. The image in Figure 11.8 can mean that I want you to loosen your association and try seeing something two different ways. Repetition also creates continuity and carves out a voice and a mental terrain.

I've used all three of the images in Figure 11.9 to promote my work. Some aren't as appropriate as others for certain audiences. I've used these three images to target three different audiences.

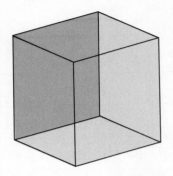

Figure 11.8 *A Repeated Image Can Create Meaning*

Know your target. For example, I use the one in the middle for teens.

> *Strategy is defined as the way in which a corporation endeavors to differentiate itself positively from its competitors, using relative corporate strengths to better satisfy customer needs.*
> —Kenichi Ohmae, *Mind of the Strategist*
> (McGraw-Hill, 1991)

Figure 11.9 *Select Images Based on Your Audience*

How Framing Paid My Way through College

I paid my way through college as a magician. I made more money than most magicians with far better hand skills. I was hired for more shows than most and was paid more for each show than most magicians could expect. I was a better showman than most magicians, but more importantly, I was a better marketer.

I would begin one routine by asking, "Are you ready to see the most amazing card trick you have ever seen in your entire life?" I would ask this seriously, and get them to promise to tell me whether the trick was the best they had ever seen. Almost always, the audience would say that it was the most amazing trick they had ever seen.

The effect of framing the trick as "the most amazing trick you have ever seen" told the audience how to view the trick. Psychological experiments have shown that telling somebody what to expect shapes their experience. For example, telling somebody they are about to taste something sweet or bland affects their experience of taste.

Your communications should tell your target audience what to expect. The effect will be sales.

My framing of the card trick affected the way people saw me as a performer. I got more shows. People would call me and say, "My friend John said that he saw you do the most amazing card trick he had ever seen in his entire life. I need you at my party." This enabled me to charge a premium for my services. Now, that's magic!

EXERCISE 11

Do you give your customers a repeatable phrase that frames your product or service well? Do you give them this framing on the packaging so they have it in their head when they first touch your product?

_____

_____

_____

_____

_____

_____

12 | Creativity on Demand: Why Ad Agencies Can't Brainstorm

B rainstorming with a professional creative is a little like playing scales with a jazz musician: The process isn't bringing out the best in either of you. First, creatives have internalized many of the basics of brainstorming. Second, most agency-led brainstorming sessions don't adhere to the fundamental guidelines set up by the man who coined the word.

Kennesaw State University's Center for Creativity and Innovation teaches creativity on demand to their MBA students and to business folks across the country. The program, called "Creativity On Demand Environment (C.O.D.E.)," drives home how to manage focused chaos—in other words, turning corporate initiatives into actions, helping teams work better together, and coming up with innovative ideas to better compete in a "flat world." Applied creativity is the backbone to innovation.

Professor Gary Selden and creativity expert Harry Vardis teach how to:

- Increase the quantity of ideas you can generate by 4 to 12 times.
- Enhance the applicability of new ideas.
- Evaluate and improve ideas through the development process.
- Identify the type of creativity that is most productive for different phases in bringing an idea to market.

Harry Vardis' book, *Potatoes? Not Yet! 33 Ways to Grow and Harvest Your Best Ideas* (J & B Publishers, 2005), captures the principles of creative problem solving and can give you insights on how to get the most out of your teams. The banana exercise in the previous chapter is from their class.

I've helped teach this class for the last couple of years by explaining to the students that their assumptions are what holds them back. I've taught them how to go beyond the obvious and look at the assumptions by changing perspectives. We see students more than quadruple their ability to generate lists of ideas in less than an hour. How do we do this? Magic fairy dust, of course. That, and we simply request participants to turn off their judging for a period of time.

We also immediately give them two brainstorming tools that are done in a group with Post-it notes:

1. *Brainstorming with Post-its*. Give everybody a pad of Post-it notes and ask them to write their ideas down and hand them in as fast as they can—but the assignment is to keep writing, even if they are just writing "I'm stuck." Any novel idea is allowed, and others are allowed to write down any idea even if somebody else said it. Just keep writing!

2. *Brain writing.* Prepare several sheets of paper with six Post-its on each side of the page. Everybody starts by writing two ideas on the top of a page and passing that page into the center of the table. They then take a different sheet from the center of the table. As you take your next sheet of paper you are open to either build on an idea on that sheet or write a new idea. You need a few sheets prepared for each person. This exercise does not require a facilitator saying them out loud until the allotted time is through, but a facilitator should be encouraging the group to keep writing. How long? You choose—say five minutes?

Do you see a commonality in those two exercises? Just write. The best way to create something is to start creating. Many people are hesitant to share ideas out loud, so writing helps them generate more ideas than they ever had before, on their own, just listing them on a single sheet of paper. Yes, many of the ideas are silly, but this is good. Silliness helps the creative process.

Everybody is creative. At some point our educational system convinced kids they weren't creative. From my experience in these classes, about half the students would label themselves as "not creative." Harry, along with other creativity experts, suggests that it is not a matter of "How creative are you?" but "How *are you* creative?"

Each of us has a different way of expressing our creative self. This is very important when forming teams so that the team is formed according to objectives and the preferences of the members. Harry explains that if you want 200 ideas in 24 hours, you should get a group of "Ideators" together and give them the challenge to work on. If you put together a team of "Clarifiers," all you are going to get in 24 hours is 100 different ways of looking at the problem. Somehow many folks view creativity exclusively as the ability to generate lists of ideas. Innovation involves more than just having a novel idea—innovation is about making a novel idea useful because it meets certain criteria.

We all have preferences. Do you prefer to:

- Clarify a problem? Do you like asking questions and delineating distinctions?

- Ideate on a problem? Are you raring to generate lists of possibilities?

- Develop plans? Do you get anxious when action isn't being planned out or when you see plans that have gaping holes in them?

- Implement existing plans? Do you love bringing ideas to fruition and get satisfaction from making something work as it was intended?

Knowing yourself helps ease you through the innovation process, both in knowing where you need help and knowing when it's your turn to shut up. More about these distinctions can be found at www.FourSight.com.

Creativity legend Alex Faickney Osborn postulated, and others have proven, that separating divergent thinking from convergent thinking will substantively improve the quality of ideas generated. (See Figure 12.1.) You start with an objective and flesh out a bunch of possibilities for this objective. Then you reach a saturation point and you say *enough*, and you begin culling and improving and narrowing your idea until you have an action plan with specific tactics.

Figure 12.1 *Separating Divergent from Convergent Thinking*

Step 1: Divergent Thinking

The first rule of divergent thinking is to defer judgment. We'll get to that in a minute. The most impressive part of the class for many is when we teach them in very short order how to quadruple the number of ideas they can generate on demand. Suddenly increasing one's ability to generate ideas isn't brand-new technology—it's just under utilized. The "O" in BBDO stands for Osborn—Alex Faickney Osborn, the guy who coined the word *brainstorming*. Here's the funny part: when I worked as a senior vice president at BBDO I never saw anybody run their brainstorming sessions as Osborn suggested was optimal, despite Wikipedia's assertion to the contrary. In fact, at the seven advertising agencies I've worked at, I never saw a "brainstorming" session run along the simple guidelines Osborn outlined in *Your Creative Power*, a book he published in 1948.

Osborne offered four rules for divergent thinking:

1.   Defer judgment.
2.   Strive for quantity.
3.   Seek wild and unusual ideas.
4.   Build on ideas.

I hear an agency account executive cursing me. "I tell my groups to defer judgment: I begin my brainstorming sessions saying that there are no bad ideas." Yeah, well how's that working for you? There are bad ideas. This is about innovation and applied creativity. This isn't self-expression and finger painting for pleasure. We're here to make money. Some ideas are more likely than others to help us make money.

A typical brainstorming session at an ad agency would go something like this: The brainstorming facilitator says, "Our client spent $3 million on a sponsorship for the Masters golf tournament and this means that we get to run an 'event' with the audience that will run after the 9th hole. What should we do? There are no bad ideas. What do you think?"

Now, a situation is helpful, damn helpful. But we need focus and clarity before we go hog wild on ideas. The notion of deferring judgment isn't quite the same thing as saying there are no bad ideas.

Effective Brainstorming

Start by stating the objective and coming up with 20 ways in which we might meet that objective. *Start with an objective*—that's key! This is applied creativity. We don't need to be drill sergeants, but we aren't doing this for the joy of playing with ideas, either. Without an objective, without direction, we flounder.

Maybe there isn't a specific objective yet. In that case, a *first step* would be to establish an objective: "Our client spent $3 million on a sponsorship for the Masters golf tournament and this means that we get to run an 'event' with the audience that will run after the 9th hole. What would be a beneficial outcome for this game? What do we want the viewer at home to experience from watching this event?"

This will deeply engage the clarifiers. Create a list of possible objectives. Then for each objective, ask the group, "In what ways might we (insert objective)?"

Now, while you're doing this, defer judgment.

- Instead of saying, "That's stupid," say, "That's different."
- Instead of saying, "We can't do that," try reframing the question: "Great. Now, in what ways might we (insert objective) for less than $20,000 ?"
- Instead of saying, "No, but . . ." say, "Yes, and . . ."
- Instead of saying, "No, we can't," say, "How can we . . .?" or "How to . . .?"

Ask open-ended questions. The facilitator of the brainstorming session should be asking about *possibilities* "How might . . . ?" Ask about target audiences, product attributes, and benefits. If a new target audience is discovered, then what product attributes are they appreciating? Why? What benefit would they enjoy? Allow for absurdity. And push for the absurd. What if we were targeting cows? (Yeah, I know cows can't read—just flow with this, let go and have fun.) If we targeted cows, what would we be saying? Why do they appreciate our product? What's the benefit to them? Is that a new benefit? What other target audiences would gain from this benefit?

Three things to listen for:

1.   New target audiences.
2.   New important product attributes.
3.   New product benefits which satisfy some need.

Here's the thing: Your first 20 ideas are often predictable. Your next 20 ideas are often just quirky, and then in the next 20 ideas are usually some juicy, usable nuggets. Can you generate 60 ideas in a single sitting? Yes—and more. Recently, I worked with Harry Vardis on a brainstorming project for a large soda manufacturer that is based here in Atlanta. In three hours a team of 14 people generated nearly 400 ideas.

The "obvious ideas, quirky ideas, juicy ideas" cycle repeats itself, but it's not very predictable in terms of number of ideas. The point is that you need to push hard and work yourself and your group to get more and more ideas. Quantity does produce quality.

You will keep your momentum if you ask "What else?" instead of "Any more?" We will often say no if given the chance. Don't ask "yes" and "no" questions.

When the group runs out of steam, give them a task: Open a magazine and look for the first picture not of a human. Look at this picture.

- What does this do?

- What are the benefits of that?

- How can we have similar benefits with our product?

- Who is this product designed for?

- How might we appeal to them? If we did appeal to this target audience, who else might we appeal to?

Step 2: Convergent Thinking

When you are finished generating possibilities, it is time to start organizing your options—the "Convergent" half of Figure 12.1. As with divergent thinking, there are four rules of convergence:

1. Be positive.

2. Be deliberate.

3. Check your objectives.

4. Consider novelty.

Applied creativity is not a "like it, don't like it" game. This is about making money. This is not about art. We have an agenda. What's our agenda again? What's the real purpose of this creative task? And don't say it's to make more money. In what way are we making more money? One of those answers gave us an objective. Looking at a given prospective solution, ask, does this prospective solution enhance the likelihood of this possibility?

Here are a couple of tools.

Bull's Eye

Either you created your ideas on Post-its, or now is the time to transfer them to Post-its. Now, place each idea on a bull's-eye like the one shown in Figure 12.2. Put ideas you see as spot-on in the center of

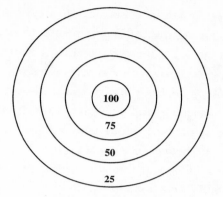

Figure 12.2   *Use a Bull's-Eye as a Tool in Convergent Thinking*

the bull's-eye. Then put the rest of the ideas in other rings. Just go with your gut. This isn't an exact science but a down-and-dirty sorting mechanism.

Okay, now anything that's not a 100, ask, "In what ways could we improve this idea to make it more powerful, likeable, attractive?" Notice the exact words are not important. This is just a down-and-dirty sorting mechanism that also enables asking how we can improve on ideas.

Matrix Evaluation

Take the Post-its from both the 75 and 100 areas of the bull's-eye. Or, if you have a lot in the 100 area, then just use those ideas. Now, let's get granular about our objectives.

You had a major objective. You probably also have other considerations.

Let's pretend we worked at BBDO on Cingular today, with their tagline of "raising the bar," and we're brainstorming because our client spent $3 million on a sponsorship for the Masters golf tournament, which means that we get to run an "event" with the audience that will run after the 9th hole. Let's say our objective is to reinforce the concept of "raising the bar" while people are having fun. First off, that's complicated, but most groups have a hard time defining a single objective, so let's play with this convoluted objective.

What is "raising the bar"? You've talked this over before, when you defined the objective, and you know from your brand essence material that raising the bar is about increased quality, mostly through better reception and better voice quality.

In generating ideas, you find three ideas that, after being enhanced, are in the 100 inner circle:

1. Game: A chip shot over a bar to land on the green; the person who hits it over the highest level of a bar wins a prize.

2. A social in the golf course's bar with a banner that says "Raising the bar!" and the announcers recap the highlight shots of the day's competition.

3. A spectacle of "Telephone" where participants are in remote places on the course and receive a call and repeat a phrase, and if the same phrase comes back as went out they all win a prize.

Table 12.1 **Rate the Ideas According to Essential Criteria**

	Easy to Get "Raising the Bar"	Involves a Handset	Memorable, Novel, Distinctive	Communicates Better Reception	Total Score
Game: Chip Shot	5	1	5	1	12
Social in Bar with Day's Highlights	2	1	3	1	7
"Telephone" Spectacle	2	5	1	5	13

Now you agree on more criteria. It would have been handy to have the list in Table 12.1 when you first started, but usually this list isn't fleshed out until you have begun generating ideas. Don't worry. You can always ask, "In what ways might we . . . ?" Using the criteria in this table, rate the three possible events on a scale of 1 to 5, with 5 being the best.

Based on this scoring, the "Telephone" Spectacle is your winner, but maybe these criteria aren't all equal. Next we create a weighting system that indicates, on a scale of 1 to 5, how important each of these criteria is. Now, multiply the score by this weighting. The results are shown in Table 12.2.

Now the Chip Shot game is our winner. Your gut is to be trusted. These are just tools to help you work through decisions and uncover considerations. One idea might simply feel right. I suggest you trust your gut. However, I believe that ease of communication is of paramount importance.

When I was at Deutsch I worked on Baskin-Robbins, a company that constantly did new product development research. They came up with a hot-cookie and ice cream sundae that I loved—scrumptious! The product would entail franchisees buying a mini-oven to bake the

Table 12.2

	Easy to Get "Raising the Bar"	Involves a Handset	Memorable, Novel, Distinctive	Communicates Better Reception	Total Score
Weighting Factor	5	3	3	2	
Game: Chip Shot	(5) 25	(1) 3	(5) 15	(1) 2	45
Social in Bar with Day's Highlights	(2) 10	(1) 3	(3) 9	(1) 2	24
"Telephone" Spectacle	(2) 10	(5) 15	(1) 3	(5) 10	38

cookies, but that would be a minor consideration if we had a hit. Research scores showed that based on name and description, folks weren't that interested in this product—but once they tried it they needed to have another, or at least planned on having another. The taste rating and planned purchase rating were off the charts! The product was launched and quickly failed.

We never overcame the communication roadblock. People won't try what they can't absorb. Yes, we absorb ideas. Ideas infect our mind. I'd rather have a very contagious idea to reach more people than an obtuse idea that only penetrates a few but does so more substantively. If that product was to be successful we needed to break out of the typical way that we had been promoting other products—a hanging sign. We needed some sort of sampling promotion, or maybe a taste guarantee. This was a perfect couponing opportunity, or a way to "Celebrate Presidents' Day with Cookies and Ice Cream." We needed an excuse to get folks trying this scrumptious delight and the word of mouth might then have taken hold.

The good news is that this type of thinking has tools that you can use. The bad news is that there isn't a blueprint for success. These tools are for you to draft your own blueprint.

I wholeheartedly endorse Mark Joyner's www.simpleology.com because he offers tools to empower people to get what they want. It is the best, most concentrated toolbox I have found, and the entire first course is completely free. Applying that first course to your company is also completely viable. Pretend your company is a person and apply goal-setting and consistency-increasing tools to your company. That's branding: upping your effectiveness through increased intentionality.

Mark Joyner sends out a weekday e-mail for Simpleology. One e-mail asked who said, "Every revolutionary idea seems to evoke three stages of reaction. They may be summed up by the phrases: (1) It's completely impossible. (2) It's possible, but it's not worth doing. (3) I said it was a good idea all along."

The answer is Arthur C. Clarke, but the point Mark is making, and the structure in which he is illustrating his points, is what I'll close out this chapter with.

Mark is teaching folks how to do the impossible. This could be thought of as magic, but *magic* is just a label like *UFO*, a label that helps us process what we don't understand. I like one quote that you read earlier in this book, also from Arthur C. Clarke—just like J. K. Rowling, I'm not afraid to repeat important ideas: "Any sufficiently advanced technology is indistinguishable from magic."

In working with creativity experts for the last two years, I've spent time on this issue. They label it *creative problem solving*. When approaching something that at first feels/appears impossible, these creativity experts ask, "In what ways might we _____?" The blank is filled in with a specific goal that may contribute toward a working solution. This may sound like hedging the task, but an indirect approach often proves useful.

A real key to successful problem solving is regularly discussed in Simpleology: focus. A focused objective is key to consistent effective problem solving.

How many times have you been invited to a brainstorming session and been told that there are no bad ideas? Bunk! Yes, in the process of brainstorming we shouldn't slow ourselves down by judging—that much is true. Please follow Osborn's first law of brainstorming: Defer judgment. But judgment will come and ideas will be deemed unusable. So how do we increase our productivity while brainstorming, without diminishing our momentum? Focus. We focus by asking a guiding question: In what way might we _____?

I use this magic—I mean technology—all the time. You see, I'm a fan of magic. I've been fascinated by magic since I was four, when a seven-year-old girl named Betsy Black in Brentwood, California, got a magic kit for Christmas. In the play cottage in the backyard of her parents' mansion, she showed me every trick in that kit several times. Sorry, you didn't need all those details, but I've always wanted to thank her. Thank you, Betsy!

Yet for many, *magic* is a dirty word. I was truly bewildered the first time a student said to me that her mom was praying for me because I was studying the tools of the devil. Card tricks—a tool of the devil? Yes. Her mom was really praying for me. On the bus ride home from school that day I made out with this girl. She must have told her mom because she was transferred to another school bus. I'm confident her mom really thought I was a devil child. They're card tricks. Magic is fun. It's like hallucinogens without the drugs.

I see my enjoyment of advertising as an extension of my interest in magic: playing with perception.

Mark's Simpleology is white magic. He is revealing tools and techniques that help unlock our talents.

Want to understand branding? Just do the Simpleology exercises for your company instead of yourself. Presto, you have branding. Some of you are saying, "But, many of the Simpleology exercises are about making me money, and aren't I already doing this?" Yes, *and* if you personify your company and think of it as a separate entity you will get different results because your ego and identification will be less entwined.

Branding is about sustaining the focus of your money-making construct. Marketing is the legitimate face of magic.

Think Piece

Buckminster Fuller's 1964 definition of *pattern integrity* is curiously similar to many current definitions of a brand: "Pattern integrity is when a pattern has integrity independent of the medium by virtue of which you have received the information that it exists" (*Synergetics: Explorations in the Geometry of Thinking*, Macmillan, 1975). If we replace the word *pattern* with the word *brand* we create the statement: "A brand has integrity independent of the medium by which you have received the information that it exists." A brand has integrity independent of the product, product name, product logo, advertisements, or any other brand accessory.

By the way, do me a personal favor: For the love of Bucky, please stop employing the word *synergy* to mean increased profits. R. Buckminster Fuller coined the word *synergy*. "We need more synergy" is a phrase I have heard too many times. Synergy does *not* mean increased productivity. Synergy means that a system has *restructured*. Restructuring may increase productivity; then again, it may not. Freezing water restructures the water molecule, which is great if your goal is stability or cold but counterproductive if your goal is fluidity.

The next chapter energizes your pattern integrity. Remember, your brand is your relationship with customers, and unless you are energizing them to buy, this is all pointless mental gymnastics. Energy—we're harnessing and redirecting energy.

Creativity Credits Provided by Harry Vardis

- Brainwriting: Introduced by Horst Geschka in *Methods and Organization of Idea Generation*. In S. Gryskiewicz, (Ed.), *Creativity Development Week* II (pp. 49–61) (Greensboro, NC: Center for Creative Leadership).

- Forced connections: Created by Charles S. Whiting; first appeared in Alex Osborn, *Applied Imagination* (New York: Charles Scribner's Sons, 1963).

- Morphological matrix: Created by Dr. Fritz Zwicky.

- Divergence rules: Alex Osborn, *Applied Imagination*.

- Convergence rules: Proposed concept of rules by Scott Isaksen and Don Treffinger in *Creative Problem Solving, the Basic Course* (Buffalo, NY: Bearly Ltd, 1985).

- Highlighting, dots and clusters: First mentioned by Don Treffinger and Roger Firestien in 1983, and developed by Multiple Resource Associates.

- Evaluation matrix: Sidney Parnes used it in his *Creative Behavior Guidebook* (New York: Charles Scribner's Sons, 1977) and *Creative Behavior Workbook* (1967).

13

Feed Their Passions

Strutting is profitable. Being controversial is appropriate for an underdog challenger brand. In your branding, I suggest you go bigger than what you are comfortable with. Common is boring. Be extraordinary.

Swagger, baby! Put some funk in your words, your packaging, and your life. I shouldn't blog or write when I'm angry or feeling unhappy. Why? Because it seeps into my words. Your attitude permeates your communications. Smile. Now, have fun with these energies. (See Figure 13.1.)

When I worked in advertising, brand managers were often the creatives' worse enemy. Why? They were too close to their product. Very, *very* few buyers care that the 1999 Galant's grill is angled differently. This isn't exciting. It isn't sexy—except perhaps to people who know cars in such detail that your advertising really isn't swaying them. Whether you make your own marketing material or somebody else does, let it swagger. Give me some panache.

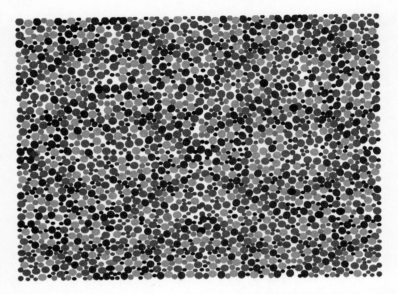

Figure 13.1 *How Much Swagger Is Right for You? Choose Your Swagger at: www.ThinkTwoProductsAhead.com/swagger*

Love and sin are extraordinary energies. Love and sin are *motivators*. We are driven by our passions. So leverage passion. Give people your passion. Give them something to talk about. People love to talk.

Dale Carnegie suggests that the easiest way to be fascinating is to be fascinated by the person with whom you are talking. Letting them talk makes you interesting. Most folks find this tough to do in advertising and packaging—listening to the buyer.

How else can we be fascinating? I learned the key to being fascinating from modern persuasion expert Blair Warren. The most powerful sentence I have ever read explains being fascinating more accurately than I have found anyplace else. The author of this sentence, Blair Warren, has sold this sentence for $97, and just to make sure his buyers appreciate the sentence he has a 12-page preface. In fact, I still suggest you go to www.BlairWarren.com and download his now free "One-Sentence Persuasion Manual" because I'm not going to do it justice here—you won't appreciate this sentence as much as I think every marketer should: "People will do anything for those who encourage their dreams, justify their failures, allay their fears, confirm their suspicions and help them throw rocks at their enemies."

How does this help you be fascinating? Continuously reinforce how you are encouraging their dreams, justifying their failures, allaying their fears, confirming their suspicions or throwing rocks at their enemies. This is how you hold their attention. This is how you are fascinating. This is why they give you their money.

Look at any of your communications, especially a secondary communication like packaging. Think of your target. Is there a way for this communication to do a better job at any of these:

- Encouraging their dreams.
- Justifying their failures.
- Allaying their fears.
- Confirming their suspicions.
- Throwing rocks at their enemies.

By validating their feelings we are demonstrating that we are listening to them. Not only that, we aren't interrupting them. How do we listen to our customers on our packaging? We reflect their values and sensibilities. Many times this entails shutting up and allowing more blank space. It is always done with respect. The more deeply we bond with our customer, the more they will prefer us to our competition. Having this conversation with your target helps them feel more alive as it makes you more money in the long run. Your communications will have a deeper resonance with your customers. They will seek you out. You become an energy they crave.

There are many types of stories. The best kind of story a brand manager can overhear ends with somebody saying that they want to buy the service or product. Trying to comprehensively classify stories would be a Herculean task, if not impossible. Stories are slippery little buggers. They keep changing. Stories are not neatly divisible into mutually exclusive, completely exhaustive rubrics. So instead, I've focused on legends.

What are legends? Legends are larger-than-life stories that are told and retold, have a meaningful connection with an audience, and grow stronger as they age. Legends are stories that have almost achieved mythic proportions. Legends are stable. They are well enough known that if a day goes by and nobody tells the story, the legend still exists. A single legend can have multiple stories, like Paul Bunyan.

A neat thing about a legend is that a single legend may contain contradictory stories. Celebrities are like modern-day legends. Stories in the press about a celebrity often contradict one another.

Brand name awareness is less a battle for *truth* than it is a battle for *prominence*. The old adage, "There is no such thing as bad press" is not entirely true. Sales do go down after a high-profile negative story about a company. However, it is generally easier to combat a bad story than it is to build awareness from scratch. (In 2005 I was ridiculed on crapauthors.com at the same time a British news site, RINF.com, bashed my work. The net result? I sold more copies of *Poker Without Cards* (lulu.com, June 2005) than I had with any of my planned publicity.)

Your brand accessories are celebrities. You're hoping they get exposure, are spoken about online, are written about in magazines, and are featured in movies. And to supplement this exposure, you produce your own media (advertisements) with your product facilitating the heroic act of a customer.

Your customer is your hero. Authentically help them and they will help you.

One of my heroes is Art Reid. Yes, he is a client of mine. More importantly, he's a friend. I wrote a book about him called *The Art*

Reid Story. (However, this book was only disseminated virally online as a file titled: FreeBookWorthReading.doc. Google will help you locate a copy.) Art has helped me appreciate the role of the tortoise in the legend of the tortoise and the hare: The focused businessperson often enjoys greater sustained wealth than the up-and-down business person. Art reminds me to build on my existing equities. When I find myself facing a big business decision, I ask myself, "What would Art Reid do?" And if I'm not choosing what Art Reid would do, I give myself 24 hours before going ahead with my decision.

Art Reid is legendary. I'm not the only person who says Art is a solid guy. Few of my clients have I had so many conversations about. Why? Because Art Reid is *known* for being a stand-up guy with great resourcefulness. You may not have heard of him, but ask anybody in advertising in Atlanta and I bet they know him, or they aren't from around here.

Your goal might not be to get known around the globe, but you want to be known in your field and to your customers. I read a research report that said more than half of Americans didn't know the name of the company that has their mortgage. This astounds me. A company has partnered with them on a *huge* amount of money, yet this company hasn't bothered to introduce themselves in a memorable way.

Hi. I'm Ben. I'm the author that you're investing this time with. I hope you're discovering ways to apply these ideas to the sustainable growth of your own company. I want you to know that you already get the basics of branding, that by respecting your customer you will intuitively make decisions that will bond them to you. Thank you for your considerations. I'd love to know how I can make this material more actionable. Sincerely, Ben. BenMackResearch@gmail.com.

14

Plan to Have Many Conversations

When an advertisement first appears, a man does not see it; the second time he notices it; the third time he reads it; the fourth he thinks about it; the fifth he speaks to his wife about it; and the sixth or seventh time he is ready to purchase.

—P.T. Barnum

Your loyal customers each went from becoming aware of you and getting enough information to try, all the way through to preferring your product or service and being willing to pay a premium to have your product or service. They followed this 10-step path to loyalty:

1. Awareness
2. Familiarity
3. Overall opinion
4. Consideration
5. Intention
6. Ownership

7. Product exploration

8. Product usage

9. Repeat buying

10. Loyalist—will buy nothing else

A great Direct Response letter takes a stranger from introduction to ownership in a single communication. The bigger the price tag, the less likely this is to occur in a single conversation. Advertising is trying to make a sale; branding is about making this sale as well as the next two sales. If making a deal to a new customer is hurting your relationship with an existing customer, that's not being good to your gander. This tactic might be costing you future sales.

Some business folks think branding means just being warm and fuzzy. I don't know where they got this misinformation. Some marketers equate the narrative in an ad as wasted space. I beg to differ. The story is part of what makes you likeable, what gets somebody's attention, what facilitates their ability to dream. Now, should you ask for a sale? Yes. Should you offer an incentive for folks who are just signing up now? Probably. Should you make a current buyer say, "If only I'd waited"? No. Because next time you approach them they will likely hesitate, knowing that a better deal is just right around the corner.

Most companies attempt to separate their conversations into two groups: users and prospects, also known as owners and nonowners. An example of this when you call a company and it asks you for to press "1" for sales and "2" for existing customers, and then the wait message has different information.

Prospects	Users
Awareness	Ownership
Familiarity	Product exploration
Overall opinion	Product usage

Consideration	Repeat buying
Intention	Loyalist who will buy nothing else
Ownership	

It feels weird for me to get a "Dear Valued Customer" letter when I've never made a purchase. Worse, I get spam that reads, "Dear _____, You are a valued customer . . ." Funny. I don't feel that valued.

If you are alone with a nonuser, then you can offer them whatever you want without current users feeling jealous. Just realize that if they are only buying now because of a steep discount, then this patron is likely to only buy with steep discounts. If you think two sales ahead, is this customer worth the effort? Will you profit enough from them?

It generally takes more than one conversation to make a sale. The neat thing about legends is that a single legend includes a multitude of stories. Structurally, an advertising campaign with more than one story is a legend. However, part of what makes legends so appealing is that they vary from one telling to the next. I have yet to see this taken into account with mass media. Sometimes I watch niche media and I might see a cool Altoids commercial during each break. It is really cool the first 8 times I see it. I might even enjoy the next 20 if there was a modicum of variation: a different expression when the guy falls in the fire, a couple of different lines here or there—anything. Eventually, I just tune it out. Slight variation gives me something to experience.

Buyers. That's what business is about—buyers. We made an offer and somebody not only said yes, they paid and we got the money in our account. For most marketers, their most expensive cost is getting a prospect to buy. Then, the moment that the customer has the product in their hot little hands, they are greeted by the conversation that has the least thought and care that has gone into the whole deal: the packaging. Opening the product is probably the most important moment in the customer's experience and has the greatest impact on their future satisfaction.

Buyers are so wonderful. They're more likely to buy from you in the future than any other target population. It's time to help them appreciate what they have. Sure, a catalogue of other offerings is fine, but your collateral about their current purchase should be all about why they made a fantastic choice and how much they will enjoy this purchase for time to come. Reinforce their belief that they've made a great purchase. Point out what's likeable.

Sometimes I buy a product and the instruction manual is almost incomprehensible, but there is a ton about what else I might buy in the future. That's sort of like screwing a girl and asking her out for next week and she hasn't had an orgasm yet.

Skip the next paragraph if you find seduction discomfiting. Be an adult.

> The truth is, the majority of people are very reasonable. They don't write letters when something offends them on TV. 'Cause reasonable people know that IT'S JUST F*C#ING TELEVISION! And not only that, reasonable people HAVE A LIFE!
>
> *Bill Hicks*

If seduction analogies don't scare you, read *The Game* by Neal Straus (Regan Books, 2005). It's all about speed seduction. Actually, it's more than that, but if you are in the business of marketing you are in the persuasion game and you are seducing customers. How do you make somebody want to sleep with you again? You ask them, "Do you like this? How about this?" and you listen to their responses, which aren't always in English. And you give them what they like.

I love hate mail. This is not an invitation. I'm just saying that having an advertisement that made somebody take some action shows that at least some people are reading your messages. If you aren't being bold you're probably invisible.

Without promotion something terrible happens. Nothing.

P.T. Barnum

I'm a huge fan of promotions. I also think that the promotion should be an extension of your brand essence; a promotion should *reinforce* your brand essence. Your story is what wraps the promotion into your brand essence, into the intellectual territory that makes the promotion yours. Your swagger. Your attitude. Your personality. Your brand. Your relationship with your customers and your prospects.

This is about building your relationship. Do you have a friend who, every time they call, you know will be asking for something? Asking somebody for something with every breath is not the way to build a long-term friendship. Occasionally, it is nice to have somebody just say hi—especially if it's a Christmas card or a thank you note.

Dear Reader,

Thank you for reading my book. If there is anything I can help you with, please don't hesitate to e-mail me.

Ben

Every communication leaves an impression. Branding respects the cumulative value of these impressions. Since most marketing communications are basically ignored, only a germ of an idea may get imbedded in our prospects' minds. Realize that it is a very rare germ that grows into a cold. You are exposed to thousands of germs a day. Your defenses keep the colds or other illnesses at bay. Colds come on when germs have built up faster than defenses tear them down. Your brand essence is the DNA of the mental germs you're leaving in peoples' minds after they have touched your communications. But when you actually have somebody's attention, I hope you will ask for the sale!

I am sometimes ridiculed for believing in brands after I say that a brand isn't your logo, isn't your awareness level, and isn't even something that has been found to be predictably measured with great accuracy. But I do believe in brands.

More persons, on the whole, are humbugged by believing in nothing, than by believing in too much.

P.T. Barnum

15

Everything Communicates

Choosing USPS or FedEx has a different feeling to the recipient. The medium is (part of) the message. If you are selling environmental products you'd better be using recycled packaging—I mean you'd better if you want to win the respect of this new customer.

Ever heard of Hartmann? (See Figure 15.1.)

Hartmann is a high-end luggage company that was totally swanky in the 1960s and 1970s. Here's how we used this technology at TG Madison to win their business and help them make more money.

Hartmann had great heritage, but their loyalists were dying of old age or being wooed away by new entrants to the luxury luggage scene. I'm sorry, to me Tumi is not luxury. Tumi might be a good piece of luggage, but it's hardly *fine*.

Figure 15.1 *Hartmann's Logo*

Let's talk swagger. Somebody with swagger might carry Tumi, but it isn't Tumi putting the swagger in their step. Hartmann is so fine it helps you swagger.

However, Hartmann sales were not spectacular when I was at T.G. Madison and we pitched Hartmann.

We told the people at Hartmann that they needed to get back to basics. Hartmann needed to create a sustainable positioning within the category that leveraged its emotional and rational benefits. Figure 15.2 explains this with two basic equations.

We broke down Hartmann's "rational" and "emotional" attributes as follows:

Rational	Emotional
Unparalleled performance	Reflective of me, reflective of my aspirations
Superior craftsmanship	
Constant innovation	Worldly, in-the-know, substantive, sexy
Beautiful designs	

If you order a Hartmann catalogue you can see how these ideas are woven into every page. But we went further.

Hartmann sells about one-eighth of it bags through the mail. The luggage would arrive in a standard cardboard box. Creating a printed box was going to cost too much. However, placing the bag

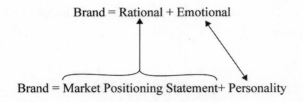

Figure 15.2 *Brand Components*

in a faux felt bag inside the cardboard box helped reinforce the specialness of the luggage of which they were just taking ownership. And we added a thank you note from the president, welcoming the owner to the heritage of Hartmann, the preferred bag of presidents.

We created in-bag collateral. On a showroom floor, many times prospective owners are showing themselves a bag. Inside the bag we placed collateral to tout the superior craftsmanship. These rational considerations were always framed in a manner that reinforced a sense of a "cosmopolitan traveler"—Hartmann's brand essence.

When a shopper is examining a bag, they are somewhere in the 10-step path to loyalty outlined in the previous chapter.

1. Awareness

2. Familiarity

3. Overall opinion

4. Consideration

5. Intention

6. Ownership

7. Product exploration

8. Product usage

9. Repeat buying

10. Loyalist—will buy nothing else

Branding is simple. Just look at everything and ask yourself if every touch a consumer has with your company or product is reinforcing your brand essence.

1. Take the 10-step path to loyalty and next to each phase write what's most important to your customer.

_____

_____
_____
_____
_____
_____
_____
_____
_____

2. Look at each element of what you wrote down and see if you can tie this in to your brand essence.

3. Now review your communications, which includes your actual product, and see where there's room for improvement.

16 | Storytelling: Letting the Genie Out of the Bottle

We learn more from stories than we do from other forms of teaching. I have seen data that proves this point for TV, and to a slightly lesser extent for radio, but not for other media. I know Direct Response practitioners have similar data. Simply making a bulleted list of attributes and slapping a price on something doesn't sell.

So if you are in sales, you're in the business of storytelling. The more the stories leverage human truths, the more likely they are to resonate with your audience. Real situations make suspension of disbelief easier because we can see ourselves in those situations. Find a way to be authentic and tell authentic stories. The stories don't need to have happened to you—but if you're writing the story, I bet it won't feel real unless you can imagine the situation happening to you.

Drama is your friend. If I am completely happy I don't need your product. Leave me alone. I don't want to be interrupted when I'm in my bliss. Fortunately for advertisers, most people aren't walking around in a state of bliss. People may be happy and want more, to feel satiated, but most people aren't even happy.

What's the most common type of story told? A love story. If you can sell love, authentic love, I suggest you do. Reinforce their love. A marketer of Elvis products asked me, "What is my brand essence?" Easy: "Long Live Elvis." Promoting "Long Live Elvis" is like saying "For people who love Elvis." I see great value in promoting love. Love helps people feel loved and unified and enfranchised and safe.

But most legends aren't love stories. Most famous legends are warnings of what can go wrong or tales of mavericks. Functionally, fairy tales often act as instructional tales for children that often scared kids away from doing things that might harm them, harm their family, or endanger their village. Legends for adults are often about a hero who solved problems in cunning ways—for instance, Paul Bunyan, Gulliver, and James Bond. Guess what—you solve a client's problem in a maverick way and they're telling their friends about you, too.

Maverick wisdom sells products. I get why John Carlton positions himself as a maverick marketer. If most of the people in the United States don't think of themselves as happy, then we'll be well served by maverick solutions. Not only does John Carlton provide maverick solutions to his clients, but the sales letters he writes frame the maverick solutions of the products being sold.

But what are these problems of ours that need solutions? Sure, there are tactical problems like needing to get from A to B, but we just do those things. Our tougher problems are getting our emotional needs met.

> When dealing with people, remember you are not dealing with creatures of logic, but with creatures of emotion, creatures bristling with prejudice and motivated by pride and vanity.
>
> —*Dale Carnegie*

Emotional creatures . . . Our problems are often unfulfilled passions. Passion sells. What emotion can you tap into? Emotions are labels for human energy. You chime an emotion and you bring forth this energy in your target.

The seven deadly sins are a decent source of energy and inspiration:

1. Pride. Bayer Advanced lawn care products sell *pride*—the pride of having a great lawn. Most lawn care companies sell pride.

2. Envy. Many products promise to make your neighbors envious of you. This makes you the object of *envy*.

3. Gluttony. Romance novels. Consume as much as you want without regrets or repercussions. A number of fake diets claim similar results with food.

4. Lust. Lust is so common that prostitutes have lost control of their market and now everybody is selling "sex."

5. Righteousness. Watch *Fox News* and feel *righteous*. Fair and balanced—we know.

6. Greed. *Fortune* magazine sells the proper face of *greed*.

7. Sloth. Corona sells "vacation." Many products sell "less work," which equals *sloth*.

Let's recap: Your narrative doesn't need to be warm and fuzzy, but you need a story to engage and bond with your customers. Even Wal-Mart has evolved from advertisements that only pound low price to commercials that tell a little bit of story.

The narrative in an effective ad reinforces your basic selling points. Whether reinforcing the reasons a person purchased or why a prospect should purchase, these are common reasons to believe your brand essence. The narrative appeals to the nonrational part of your customers. If you didn't need stories you could just send prospects your PowerPoint presentations or put the slides directly on TV. Telling a story might not seem rational, but storytelling has been proven to be a consistently effective means of persuasion.

Furthermore, you should be grateful your customers aren't more rational. You are asking something very irrational of them. You want them to be completely loyal to you while you go out there and seduce other customers. Try this one on your spouse: "Honey, I want to sleep with other people but I want you to be completely faithful to me."

Great copy is engaging. I'll read any John Carlton DR letter on golf, and I don't even play golf. I just enjoy reading his prose. Call me sick, but I like reading his words. He's a world-class storyteller. Same goes with copywriter Michael Morgan. Michael has fun with his text and I have fun when I read his words. Check it out at http://www.outsourcecopy.com.

This book, *Think Two Products Ahead*, was originally sold as an online download for $197. I know that many readers will have a difficult time imagining folks paying nearly two Benjamins for this book. Wanna read what compelled them? Everybody who paid $197 for this as an e-book read Michael Morgan's sales letter, which you can read at www.ThinkTwoProductsAhead.com/Michael_Morgan. John Wiley & Sons is innovative enough to bring an e-book to mainstream attention. I see Wiley as brave.

Being a good brander is about being a good storyteller. However, just as innovation is applied creativity and not purely self-expression, selling is applied storytelling and not simply the traditional three-act structure.

In some ways, copywriting can be seen as a morality play, where the point of the play is to teach a lesson, such as "Nobody ever got fired for choosing AT&T." In other instances, copywriting can be seen as a mystery, where the point of purchasing may be to improve your golf swing, but it is also to find out something, such as "how a one-legged golfer can drive a ball that far." For toys, copywriting can be seen as a fantasy, where the point of purchasing is to become part of the fantasy and to gain a license to be absurd: "Feel the force." For candy or alcohol, it can be a comedy: "That's brilliant!"

The other day I was in a grocery store and one 12-year-old boy said to another, "I feel like Skittles." The second kid made a sheep noise and said, "Stop that jibber-jabbing." As they walked around a corner, each grabbed a pack of Skittles. Then they started making absurd connections between things, which weren't funny to me, but they were cracking each other up. They weren't saying they were craving the flavors—they were craving the energy they associated with the product from the marketing. Skittles gave them a prop that enabled them to act a certain way. Without these props most folks just won't get that silly.

> I'm not popular enough to be different.
>
> *—Homer Simpson*

These examples I've cited of various types of stories are all from mass advertising campaigns. They tend to be inoffensive because they are big brands with big bucks, and it is a pain in the ass when some tight-ass organization starts attacking them publicly.

But most brands aren't king of the hill. Most brands are challenger brands. You have to be distinctive. I'm not suggesting you swear—that might not be your personality. If it isn't, I'm grateful you've tolerated my foul language in this text. Sincerely, thank you for putting up with my crap. I went to Fairfax High School in Los Angeles; this is how we talked. I'm attempting to keep it real.

What's funny to me is that it has been the rare CMO or CEO who would be offended if I inadvertently dropped the F-bomb. I've often heard C-level players swear in ways I hadn't heard or thought of before. It was the midlevel brand managers who got all thrown by an occasional cuss word.

Even if you don't swear, being bold and different will get you attacked. You will be attacked, whether by a colleague or a client. I would prefer to be attacked occasionally and make money than to sit against the wall and only talk to other wallflowers.

If you are bold you will attract energy, not all of which will be complimentary. You can handle this. It may be easier to handle with a few random civilians than with colleagues, bosses, and superiors. However, if you are helping them make money, I bet you will be forgiven.

I was recently challenged about whether Legendary Branding really created legends. I was at a marketing meeting. I had recently seen this woman in a much more casual setting. I knew she disliked me, though I don't know why. I knew she had waited until this moment to ask a pointed question. She had rehearsed this question and everybody in the room could feel the daggers in her voice. When she asked whether Legendary Branding really created legends, I was jolted by her energy and so was everybody else in the room. I paused before responding. Then I authentically thanked her for asking me the question.

Why was I authentically grateful? She had created drama. She created an extraordinary situation. This event was likely to be retold. It is difficult to buy that kind of opportunity. I asked if I could perform a magic trick as a reply. She seemed flustered and wanted me to answer her question. I was cool. I enjoyed the mounting energy and focus in the room because I saw this exchange as an opportunity. I performed the invisible deck trick. I got the entire group to applaud. Afterward, I explained how I made more money than other magicians with better hand-skills.

Remember earlier in this book when I told you about the most amazing card trick you would ever see in your entire life? Somebody seeing that trick then told their friends they had seen the most amazing card trick they had ever seen in their entire life. I gave them the framing—I gave them something to talk about. I made it sexy but, more importantly, I made it easy for them to share this extraordinary experience. As soon as any person told their friend my trick was the "most amazing card trick" they had ever seen in their entire life," it was legendary. A legend is a story that is repeated. The trick is that they have to be given the words to repeat.

If you are hoping to have people talk about you, then you have to give them words they can repeat, a phrase that tumbles out of their mouth. Internet discussions are different because people can cut and paste. But cut and paste usually looks like cut and paste and not an authentic conversation. To encourage folks to actually speak and/or type original conversations about your product, give them tools to help them along. This is the most amazing card trick you'll ever see in your entire life. I don't care if they parrot back the exact phrase, but if they have trouble repeating the concept, you're not going to get talked about.

Most folks are not very skilled are describing extraordinary events, let alone being extraordinary without the help of products. You gotta love 'em. It is rewarding when the kid picks up the Skittles and pretends to be a sheep. I love it when somebody describes my card trick as "the most amazing card trick I have ever seen in my entire life."

On a grumpy day I'm cynical. These are days I should not be writing copy, either as text or even most e-mails. My grumpiness permeates my writing despite how hard I try to temper my feelings. I feel smug. I feel like this:

> You gotta bear with me, I'm very tired, very tired of traveling, and very tired of doing comedy, and very tired of staring out at your vacant faces looking back at me, wanting me to fill your empty lives with humor you couldn't possibly think of yourselves. Good evening.
> —*Bill Hicks, patron saint of comedy*

I *love* Bill Hicks. And he died broke. He died of cancer that might have been curable if he'd had health insurance and had gone to a doctor much sooner. I thank Bill for providing an example for me. Bitterness doesn't make money. Bitterness is not attractive energy. Righteousness isn't attractive.

I mentioned marketing rebel John Carlton earlier. John Carlton illustrated this point by contrasting the folks who invented neurolinguistic programming (NLP) to a famous seminar leader who made millions teaching people these ideas in the 1980s. The PhDs who invented it won awards but were bitter. They didn't have people flocking to them. They could even show how the famous guru was teaching, wrong, but they couldn't understand why folks didn't want to learn from them.

I do. Their righteous indignation kept folks away. Righteous indignation is girl repellant. Not sexy. But eventually, the NLP guys all got rich. Anthony Robbins is wealthy.

I've learned to get negativity out of my system before entering a business meeting and before writing e-mails—most of it, anyway. I'm sorry to drag you down with me in my moments of weakness.

I know how to do church—how to dress up and mind my manners and my language. I worked a gig for Coca-Cola recently—not exactly the corporate audience that laughs at synonyms for *crap* in the big meetings. But they dig it over a beer. And we laugh together. I know their pain of having to perform a presentation with an insight that doesn't really work. But the presentation was developed separately from the insight team, and—well, the insight is still valuable. I don't blame them for being in that jam. I feel their pain. I've been there. That's why I made up the word *intellishit*.

At big agencies I've seen creative teams that loathe a target audience. You know what happened: The ads sucked. Of course they did. You gotta love your target and speak to them when you're feeling the love.

Folks can't make up what to say about you. Don't make fun of them for their lack of originality. Rather, discover what they can repeat, and help them repeat those words.

These are your customers, folks. They're feeding your children. You gotta love 'em.

17 | Branding and Thinking Two Products Ahead

Thinking is a verb, requiring action—work. The good thing about this work is that it makes many of your later choices easier and more intuitive.

Science fiction authors Kurt Vonnegut and Philip K. Dick both used recurring characters in various novels. When asked why, each of them said that they already knew those characters so they knew how to write them. That's what you're doing with this work: You're getting to know your public face and developing that character to yield you more money.

Branding is about developing a relationship and enchanting your customer—and sustaining that enchantment through when they are ready to buy again.

Here's a case where that didn't work. I recently bought a copy of *The Chemical Wedding of Christian Rosencreutz*, the sixteenth century text the *Harry Potter* series is purported to be based on. I had already downloaded the text for free, but I wanted to give the book as a gift to a friend for his birthday. So I paid $33 to "Alex" for a leather-bound copy of the book. Alex was entrepreneurial enough to have read a post of mine referencing the manuscript. I'll use the name Alex because maybe he has a good product now. I was impressed with the young man's hustle, and I PayPal'ed him the money.

I doubt I'll do business with him again. The leatherette cover feels cheap and the book came late. I e-mailed him that I was disgruntled. To his credit, he apologized for the product being late, but I still feel burned and I don't trust him or his company to provide quality products. If the binding were only decent, I bet I would have gone to Alex's web site first when considering gifts for the more esoteric of my friends. But no, I had to scramble and get a last-minute gift because his product was late. On top of that, what did arrive I would have been embarrassed to give even if it had arrived on time.

Why do that? How much does real leather cost? I found some at the local Michael's craft store for $6, and it was enough to cover two books. I would have gladly paid $50 for the book if it had been really cool, on something that looked like aged paper with a hand-stitched leather binding.

If I were selling leather bound copies of *Chemical Wedding*—selling esoteric knowledge—I'd be writing a report on how you can see the tools from *Chemical Wedding* in the *Harry Potter* series and selling that to buyers of *Chemical Wedding*, and sending DR letters to folks who dug *Harry Potter*. Then I might figure out a third product that tied these products together or leveraged the equities of those texts for another text or product of some sort. This is *thinking two products ahead*. The work done on the previous pages of this book would help steer the products and communications down a familiar path.

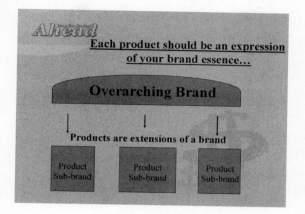

Figure 17.1 *Relationship between Brand and Product*

Your brand is your relationship with a prospect. Figure 17.1 shows the relationship between your brand and your products.

As a side note, a group of women at Clif Bar recognized a need for a nutrition bar for women—not necessarily a sports bar, but a nutrition bar full of vitamins and minerals for women. This isn't exactly "fuel" to help somebody do something athletic, and it was just for women, so this idea never became a Clif Bar but, instead, a Luna Bar by Clif.

If somebody has a good experience, they are open to buying again. Your biggest cost is in getting a buyer. A cost-effective way around this is to have a brand, a pre-existing relationship, so that you can short-cut part of this conversation:

1. Awareness

2. Familiarity

3. Overall opinion

4. Consideration

5. Intention

6. Ownership

7. Product exploration

8. Product usage

9. Repeat buying

10. Loyalist—will buy nothing else

If you have a brand, they will already have an opinion of you and be halfway to ownership.

Imagine a family of complimentary products. Tom's of Maine started with toothpaste and expanded into mouthwash and dental floss. I can see it continuing to expand into biodegradable soap and shampoo. Tom's of Maine sells "respect for nature," so just about anything that respects nature might be an extension of their brand.

Tom's of Maine started as "100% Natural Toothpaste," but the product platform became simply "Tom's of Maine." Tom's of Maine is about "100% Natural" hygiene products.

I hear an objection: "Ben, I'm just a JV'er. I'm not selling my own products. I don't need a brand. I just find products I think I can sell and I market those items."

At the beginning of the Industrial Revolution, production had not kept pace with demand. Railroads had connected our great nation, increasing distribution to newfound heights. Goods were produced in one region and shipped to another, either directly or through a central coordinating catalogue company. In the 1880s, three companies emerged—Sears, Roebuck & Co.; Bloomingdale's; and Montgomery Ward & Co.—profiting from this new capability of distribution. However, the contents of their catalogues were not listed as brands or by manufacturer, but by product and function. An example is shown in Figure 17.2, the index of the 1887 Sears catalogue. Note the listing of products as opposed to brands.

Figure 17.2 *Index of 1887 Sears, Roebuck & Co. Catalogue*

Ads in this era touted the function of their product, often with exaggeration. The buyers knew nothing about the manufacturer, except for possibly a name on the box or product. Many of the products ordered didn't really work, or didn't work for long. The catalogues that survived offered guarantees and screened the merchandise they sold. In such cases, the catalogue's name became a promise of quality. These retailers were the first mass consumer brands. Consumers would prefer to buy one product because it was "from Sears" as opposed to a similar product from Intellishit Marketing.

If you build trust, you have brand equity that will help make your future sale.

Afterword

Myth, Magic, and Making Money the Old-Fashioned Way

Wealthy people either inherited their wealth or created and told their own stories in order to create the wealth and life of their dreams. To the extent we tell successful stories of ourselves, success becomes easier. I've incorporated Ben Mack's technology into Bold Approach, Inc., and we leverage his technology to help our clients tell the most potent stories they can.

When my associates and I work with a new client, we seek to uncover their *brand essence*, the primary common thread we weave into every story we tell about this client. We already did this before I met Ben, but his approach of Legendary Branding has made this work easier and more consistent. Now, across a specialized marketing firm of six people, we know we are all telling complementary stories for each client. The integration of these tales builds a stronger, more compelling persona for our clients.

If you are an online genius and you can make gobs of money from your bedroom, that's great. However, the majority of us have to sell our ideas. Even Bill Gates had to sell IBM on leasing Windows from him. He didn't even own the software. The point is that IBM executives had to find his ideas compelling. Gates was getting them to buy his idea. Gates was persuading a panel of executives to trust him with their investment. He had to create a compelling story to pull that off, and clearly it worked.

This is a different way of looking at the world around us. We live in an attention economy where we are constantly persuading folks to pay attention to us and our ideas. When I hold your attention you are literally buying what I am saying. What is the greatest predictor of buying? Time spent contemplating a purchase. As a professional you are seeking to persuade more people to buy your idea, product, or service. This is *persuasion*, not coercion or manipulation.

Persuasion when done correctly creates change at a physiological, psychological and biological level in the person you are persuading. It allows them to check their internal map of what is true or not against a story that you've carefully crafted for them after eliciting their *buying criteria*—not a list of features, but a list of emotional criteria that allows them to say yes with total confidence.

What I'm about to share with you is not new. Powerful leaders have been employing this technique for thousands of years. However, this technology has not often been taught, especially not to the masses. When you begin consciously applying these techniques the results may appear magical.

How to Persuade

1.   Open with a powerful persona.
2.   Elicit information.
3.   Tell a powerful story to lead them to their own most logical conclusion.

In order to persuade effectively, you start with your persona. Much of a decision about whether to buy from you happens within seconds of meeting you and long before you have a chance to open your mouth and say your first words.

Ben's Legend Platform helps you craft and reinforce this persona. Does your costume reinforce your brand essence? And for readers surprised by my use of the word *costume*, get a clue. When you are in public and conducting business you are wearing a costume. Many businesspeople wear a uniform we call a suit. That's a fine choice. The important component is that you are making these choices.

Your persona encompasses more than your clothes, beyond the basics like freshly shined shoes and pressed clothes. Ask yourself if your hairstyle is current (note, if it is over three years old, it is probably out of date, regardless of whether you are a man or a woman). If you've gained or lost more than 10 pounds in the past year and haven't had your clothes altered or updated, they will not give you a powerful first impression. Are you dressed at the right level?

Do you want more power from your persona? You should dress at least as well as the CEO of the company you are selling to or one step better. But dressing is just the first step in analyzing your costume. There are at least a dozen other areas that you must consider, like every prop you carry on your person or in your briefcase.

The main point here is *intentionality*. Be intentional about the persona you are crafting, be intentional about the brand you are creating, and be intentional about the legend you create for your business. Ben's work gives you the timeless map for turning intention into powerfully profitable outcomes.

Simply increasing the consistency of your current presentation with the persona you desire will increase your persuasive quotient instantly. Since people are going to judge you by what they see, be sure that they see a first-rate costume. But beware: A costume that looks like a costume is a second-rate costume. In my book *Persuasion: The Art of Getting What You Want* (New York: John Wiley & Sons, 2005), you'll find a complete persona checklist that includes clothing, your voice and communication skills, and the presentation of your total package—your compete persona. Measure these elements against your brand essence. In what way might you better reinforce your brand essence?

In order to craft a powerful story that will draw people in and resonate with them in a way that makes them want to draw *your* conclusion, you must ask better questions. The questions you want to ask elicit not only product or service requirements but emotional requirements, which will be the true criteria by which your offer is judged.

To elicit emotional buying criteria you have to ask very detailed and penetrating questions. Here are a few examples of questions that will begin getting to emotional buying criteria:

- What specifically will successful implementation of this product or service mean to you personally?
- How will you define success in relation to this product or service?
- What was the final straw that made you decide to purchase this product or service or to replace your existing product or service?
- Other than you, who will be evaluating the success of this?
- If you could wave a magic wand and get exactly what you want, what would it look like? Why specifically would you want it to look like that?

When you begin asking open-ended questions that elicit emotional responses, you'll find the pain and the criteria to successfully position your solution. You've heard the old-fashioned sales training of "sell the pain"? If not, try hanging out in a mattress store some Saturday morning and listen to how the salespeople get prospective buyers to relive the pain caused by their old mattress.

How do you use people's pain and emotions? You tell a story with a moral that helps them alleviate their pain or fulfill their dreams. Morality tales lead people to draw a most logical conclusion, that there is a best path to take. We are deeply persuaded by powerful stories because they are the oldest form of communication we know. Rather than rattling off a list of features and benefits, if you tell a story about how someone else used the product's specific features and benefits, or used the service to get a similar set of results, and demonstrate it deeply by using metaphor, the person listening can draw only one conclusion—the one you want them to—but they will defend it as their own forever.

Ben's Legend Platform helps you orchestrate your stories and give them more impact in their application.

Look, persuasion is both an art and a science, but one that you must master or you will find yourself more frustrated than you deserve. Your ability to earn is in direct proportion to your ability to persuade. Persuasion truly is the art of getting what you want.

Think Two Products Ahead helps you uncover the most powerful stories you should be telling about yourself. The harder you work at making your story believable, the more you will manifest your intentional results. Your confidence will soar and, to many around you, your results will appear magical. However, there is a method to this madness, and you will have made your money the old-fashioned way—you will have earned it.

Dave Lakhani
President, Bold Approach, Inc.
Author, *Persuasion: The Art of Getting What You Want* and *The Power of an Hour: Business and Life Mastery in an Hour a Week*
www.boldapproach.com

THE END

We hope you enjoyed the fireworks. But wait, there's more!

Please go to www.ThinkTwoProductsAhead.com.

Free Bonus! Download video tutorials and MP3 case studies ($597 value).
PLUS, the first 1,023 get two FREE Passes to Direct Response Branding Boot Camp ($3,897 value).

The Appendixes that follow includes the ramblings of a scattered account planner. Proceed at your own risk. Young children should not consume these ideas unattended.

A

AKS

My Dear Reader,

I'd like to share a sad story . . . a saga of a company that owned a territory and lost its terrain. This story requires going back several years, to 1946. America is celebrating the end of World War II, pregnant women line the streets, and the world is breathing easier now that Nazism is squelched. Aside from the women, we see that much of the country is relatively sterile. There aren't many new cars, bedsheets come only in white, and there are three flavors of ice cream: vanilla, chocolate, and strawberry.

Along comes a guy named Burton who is having fun trying all sorts of different flavors of ice cream. He's even mixing chunks of stuff into ice cream. People dig it. (Okay, that's anachronistic. They didn't use the word *dig* in that way in the 1940s.)

Ice cream has always been delicious. Suddenly it's fun. Fun is often profitable: People like to have fun, especially when they're out shopping.

Burton's ice cream is fun, and demand soars. He can't keep up with demand and teams up with a guy named Irvine to help him with his business. Their business flourishes as consumers are tantalized by the kooky stuff Burton and Irvine are using to flavor ice cream. Their stores are fun and colorful. The walls have cream, brown, and pink circles on them. This is a reminder of what they evolved from, the three primary flavors of ice cream: vanilla, chocolate, and strawberry.

Sure, Burton and Irvine still had chocolate—they had seven varieties of chocolate ice cream. Who knew ice cream could be this good? As their business was formalized and they began opening stores, they put their brand essence as a subtitle to their name: Baskin-Robbins, 31 Flavors. Burton Baskin and Irvine Robbins knew that their success was being generated by their newfound creativity in ice cream flavor selection. Baskin-Robbins sales continued to grow until the late 1960s. They had several hundred formulas for ice cream, but the store was consistently called Baskin-Robbins, 31 Flavors . . . even when the store had 42 flavors on the front counter.

Baskin-Robbins, 31 Flavors stagnated in the 1960s. Worse yet, market share and constant dollar analysis have, for the most part, declined ever since, with a mild resurgence in the 1980s only to fall again.

In 1998, the Baskin-Robbins advertising campaign came up for review. The review requested that agencies explain why Baskin-Robbins had declined in sales, albeit slowly, since the late 1960s. Part of the pitch process entails uncovering a brand essence. Sometimes you can create an ad campaign on a gimmick or a category insight, but it seems that great advertising says that brand X = Y. What did Baskin-Robbins stand for? It says 31 flavors on all the signs. Cheryl Greene at Deutsch saw Baskin-Robbins as no longer owning *flavors*; Ben & Jerry's surely owned flavors. Baskin-Robbins could claim indulgence, but that seemed obtuse and not ownable—Häagen-dazs has a richer ice cream, a common barometer of indulgence.

Cheryl employed Dr. Irving Schlessinger to interview Baskin-Robbins patrons, one-on-one, with deep regressive interviewing. Many patrons associated Baskin-Robbins with their youth. Many of them recalled with fondness all the fun they had as a child going to Baskin-Robbins. In examining those memories, participants explained that it was events like going to Baskin-Robbins that made their childhoods happy. Bingo! Cheryl heard something she could work with.

Baskin-Robbins started to not work in the late 1960s, when the Vietnam War broke out. The company continued to do poorly during the whole Watergate era. It came back a little when the economy surged with Ronald Reagan, but not as strongly as its sector. What Cheryl came up with was a story that illustrated the rise and fall of Baskin-Robbins' success. Cheryl told the story of happiness—the abundance in the postwar era and its continuance through the 1960s when America lost its naïveté. This explained why Baskin-Robbins hadn't enjoyed the boom of the Reagan era: because moroseness and heroin chic were in vogue. Then she showed how happiness was an emerging fashion by quantifying the use of the words *happy* and *happiness* over the previous several years. I wasn't there, but I heard that in the end, they drove down the street to a Baskin-Robbins store decked out with their happiness campaign. "Don't worry, be happy" played on a boom box. Deutsch won the new business pitch because Deutsch was the best at answering why Baskin-Robbins had declined in sales since the 1960s.

Why did I tell you that story? I wanted to explain to you how an account planner or brand strategist can help you justify your failures. I can do that, but it feels so much better when the task is to help you make money.

Why did I frame this story as sad? Because Baskin-Robbins owned variety and then lost this terrain. Is this a big deal? Is the loss of hundreds of millions of dollars a big deal? What's the connection between variety and happiness? It is the difference between exciting and nostalgic. Other agencies had pitched nostalgia and lost. Part of the reason was that nostalgia is emotionally flat. There is no specific emotional promise in nostalgia. Deutsch said the benefit was happiness. One of the Baskin-Robbins executives asked, "Isn't happiness fleeting?" and Cheryl responded, "That's why ice cream melts."

I got sidetracked. The cost of losing variety, of losing its flavor equity, was that Baskin-Robbins lost its relevance. Variety has an implicit promise of constant reinvention, which is exciting. New fends off staid. New = Contemporary. New flavors also kept Baskin-Robbins topical as new flavors reflected contemporary issues. When Jimmy Carter was president, they had a presidential ice cream, a peanut crunch flavor. How hip was that? Okay, it was cheesy, but it was topical, which is contemporary. At a certain point Baskin-Robbins stopped doing that sort of stuff. That was the beginning of its flavor equity demise.

Had Baskin-Robbins continued to create out-there flavors, there might not have been the marketplace for Ben & Jerry's. Aside from great flavors, Ben & Jerry's borrowed from Baskin-Robbins' success and named flavors after contemporary icons, flavors like Cherry Garcia and Phish Food. Maybe Baskin-Robbins wouldn't have been that liberal, but they could have found other contemporary icons to help their ice cream stay topical and feel "now."

The challenge of Baskin-Robbins = Happiness is that advertising can carry only so much of the weight of happiness. Just because you have new ads and new posters on the wall, these accessories don't substantively change the attitude of the minimally paid coin jockey who fills your cone. Happiness is much harder to fulfill on a store level than variety. Nevertheless, happiness could have been implementable; it just would have meant buy-in from the top of the organization all the way to colleagues on the floor. A beautiful vision not endorsed by the entire team is probably a mirage.

If you shift your brand essence, buy-in will be required from store-level colleagues, directors of all divisions, and the uppermost level of management. Uppermost management buy-in is imperative; without this you won't be given the liberty or resources to see this vision to fruition. Branding becomes the corporate religion, espousing values and dictating certain actions while forbidding others. Branding saturated to this extent exists only when championed and reinforced from the top down.

Are you prepared to garner this kind of consensus? If you are in a large organization, probably not. It's nothing personal, but when there are a lot of powerful players, it is often best to have a neutral party navigate around political land mines. They have no history with these players. If they step on somebody's toes, you won't bear the grudge for the rest of your career. This is all beside the point if professional group facilitators are really good at what they do, maintain energy, and move toward appropriate consensus. One hopes these discussions get passionate. You are playing with your future, your company's future, and the financial well-being of both. In moments of tension, just remember that each of you love your brand and this tension is an expression of this common love. I mean that quite literally even though it may sound a bit airy-fairy.

Generally, a brand essence either defines what you are as a company or promises a consumer experience. However, it is possible to have a brand essence that states what you are not as opposed to what you are. In 1984, Apple Computer = Not Corporate. At least that is what its two-minute Super Bowl commercial implied.

Marketing is about re-creating yourself. Anytime somebody comes up with a rule, there are examples that run contrary to it. I would defend that a brand essence should have an emotional promise.

Amazon.com = Largest. Nothing emotional. Not an emotional ploy for wonder of reading. Nada. Largest is a perfectly valid brand essence. However, Largest = Variety implies new, so maybe there is an implicit emotional promise.

What is a good brand essence? I can't say. It seems that every generalization has many exceptions when you think about it. The category of why you do it tends to be reserved for nonprofits because these brand essences tend to sound like crusades. Some national brands, however, have done well by a crusadelike stance. This may be sustainable only until a company reaches a certain size. Laura Ashley started out as tailored clothing at reasonable prices because every professional woman deserves to dress well. When her brand grew to a certain size, it no longer felt like a benevolent act. A Los Angeles ski resort uses a mission statement brand essence with a sense of irony: Mountain High Ski Resort, because you have to ski. The ads take this idea to an extreme, but it also makes them good guys. They run their snowmakers not so that they can make money before Mother Nature says it is ski season, but because "you gotta ski."

Some would argue that Southwest Airlines has done well with Southwest = Low Fares. There is no emotional promise; there is nothing romantic about cheap. The CEO says that Southwest = Low

Fares. Low Fares is an operational directive and not a brand essence. To consumers, the advertising says that Southwest = Freedom. Freedom is the emotional benefit of low fares, because Low Fares means "I can [afford to] go there."

Let's move on. You're doing good reading all this for extra credit. This is hard work for many people because we aren't taught to think like this in school.

Whatever brand essence you extract(ed), it has to be something that will help you make money. Cingular Wireless' original brand essence was Self-Expression. This was not seen as a profitable positioning. I disagree, but I do know that Self-Expression was not a compelling idea in 2002, with the United States involved in a military buildup abroad and at home.

Self-Expression is playing pretty high up on Abraham Maslow's Hierarchy of Needs. Look at the rhombus outlining Self-Actualization

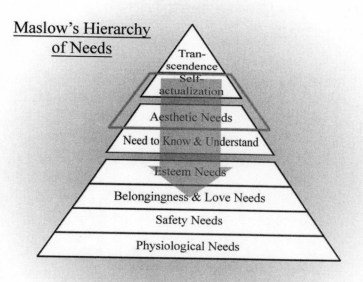

Maslow's Hierarchy of Needs

Transcendence

Self-actualization

Aesthetic Needs

Need to Know & Understand

Esteem Needs

Belongingness & Love Needs

Safety Needs

Physiological Needs

and Aesthetic Needs. This brand essence was doable, but the unper-
formed trick would have been making your message connect with the
current zeitgeist—the prevailing popular perception.

**Military actions push our zeitgeist down Maslow's Hier-
archy of Needs, as illustrated by the arrow.** Military actions
raise the stakes of life. Consumers have a heightened interest in Safety
and Belonging.

Marlboro rides through huge swings in public perceptions. The
video *The Pitch, Poker & the Public* shows Jay Levinson explaining
how the Marlboro Man took two years to catch on. But we need to
make money today. We need to drive retail sales today!

Brand Essence and Retailing

Thinking of your general brand essence, I want you to get really tactical and fill out a marketing positioning statement.

Think of a specific communication . . .

1.   Who are we selling to?
2.   What's our competition?
3.   Why will our consumer care?

Market Positioning Statement

"To (primary target audience),
BRAND is the one (competitive set)
that (meaningful point of difference)."

The "meaningful point of difference" should be an expression of your brand essence. Why your target consumers will care should be an expression of your brand's essence. The marketing positioning statement will help you focus your ideas. Your marketing positioning statement may change frequently, framing any number of specific conversations from an advertising campaign to your product's packaging.

The marketing positioning statement is the framework for your seduction. You are leveraging your strongest equity and framing this distinction so that a group of people will care tremendously about this distinction. A marketing positioning statement is the practical manifestation of a brand's essence.

After you write a marketing positioning statement, ask yourself:

Does this marketing positioning statement reinforce a sense of my brand essence?

If you find yourself fudging your brand essence, reconsider your brand essence.

For years, Diet Coke has outsold Diet Pepsi. One can argue that Coke had a stronger bonding with an audience than Pepsi had, and the disparity of Diet Coke sales to Diet Pepsi sales would support that extension. Diet Coke has stood for "great taste" while Diet Pepsi has stood for "one calorie." Which is more important to you as a diet soda drinker?

Remember the KiiC example I gave earlier? If the explicit target was teens, then the name KiiC and the draft collateral would have been spot on! The marketing positioning statement worked against teens; however, KiiC did *not* work against the larger target audience.

Before marketing communications are "concepted," the brand essence is adapted into a marketing positioning statement. *Concepted* . . . that word struck my buddy Dave Navarro as odd, but that's the word often used in creative departments. I've heard it said and that's what gets done: A concept is created. It is concepted. Usually,

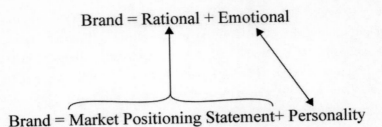

several different concepts are sketched, often scores of concepts. This phase is called concepting. Before you concept, it is helpful to have the brand essence worked into a marketing positioning statement.

The more you are able to consistently use language and images, the more familiar your communications will feel.

Your rationale for believing your brand essence is likely to change with your target audience or specific product. Your personality should be predictable and familiar.

Mitsubishi Case Study

A different example: In 1999, Deutsch advertising had won some of Mitsubishi's regional advertising business based on the brand essence of Mitsubishi Automobiles = Vitality. Deutsch created ads where a bunch of guys were working out in a gym and a page announces, "The owner of a tan minivan, you left your lights on." Those working out are scanning the room to see what wimp drives the minivan. Mitsubishi of North America chose to run these regional ads nationally instead of ads proposed by G2, its incumbent agency. G2 had been building ads around the essence of "distinctive," challenging luxurious cars. I was watching *The Simpsons* that week and saw Homer say, "I'm not popular enough to be different." In the pitch against G2, a picture of Homer saying this line appeared on Deutsch's leave-behind presentation.

While the brand essence of vitality has remained constant, Deutsch expressed this in different faces against different targets.

Mitsubishi Automobiles = Vitality	
To **aging** single **males**,	To **young** singles,
Mitsubishi is the one automobile	Mitsubishi is the one automobile
That won't make you older than you are.	**That reflects your rhythm.**

On the left is where Deutsch started; on the right is where they evolved to, fully owning a youthful positioning. At the time Volkswagen had been airing some hip ads revolving around music. But Volkswagen also ran ads where parents feel young. Volkswagen was trying to straddle youthful and family audiences. VW lost. Eric Hierschberg, Deutsch LA's creative director, outexecuted Volkswagen and maybe more importantly sent a message unwaveringly to youth or the youthful side in all of us. Hierschberg helped Mitsubishi take ownership of the segment that enjoys celebrating young energy.

How did Deutsch land on Mitsubishi Automobiles = Vitality? I can't say. It isn't that I am bound to silence. Choosing a brand essence is as much art as it is due diligence. From having been there, I know that Vitality came as an answer to the question "Where can we be?" Owning Vitality seemed to have the broadest, deepest appeal.

This appendix details the data and kinds of insights that you may consider when extracting your brand essence. A traditional way to begin synthesis is a SWOT analysis, aggregating all relevant ideas into four basic buckets: strengths, weaknesses, opportunities, and threats.

Obviously, if you do this exercise with modicum of diligence, your list will far exceed the space available on a single sheet of paper. It will probably take several sheets of paper for each rubric.

Part of what helps generate lists of strengths, weaknesses, opportunities, and threats is having a long list of considerations. The list of considerations I include in this chapter is downloadable at

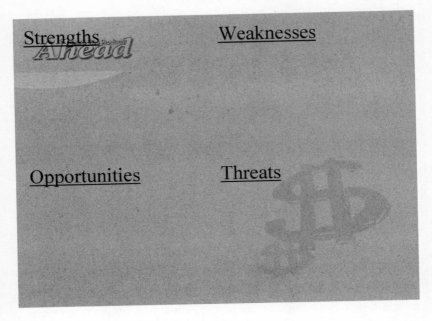

www.ThinkTwoProductsAhead.com. Downloading these considerations may be helpful when you are brainstorming alone or with colleagues on these topics.

Start with the end in mind and work backwards. First look at some of the outcomes of synthesis; then look at specific considerations. When you are done with synthesizing all your data, you should be able to identify:

- Emotional drivers of core constituents of where we want to be.
- Emotional drivers of current core constituents.
- Emotional impact on patrons.
- Perceived implication of being a patron.
- Equities and liabilities of an imagistic landscape such as logo and design.

- Perceived equities and liabilities of a product.
- Perceived future role of its category.
- Possible avenues to strengthen your current image.

Your brand essence should be large enough to be thoroughly satisfying to the larger target to whom you hope to appeal. Interspersed between sections of this list are some of the details and considerations that led Deutsch to land on Vitality.

Brand Analysis

- Awareness: our brand vs. competitive landscape.
- Bonding: our brand vs. competitive landscape.
- Brand heritage.
- Brand associations: our brand vs. competitive landscape.
- Possible larger spaces for brand to live.
- Needs for brand extensions.
- Identification of brand extension outliers.

Mitsubishi had high total awareness, but so did every established car manufacturer. The weakness of the public's awareness was evident when consumers were asked,

"When you think of brands of cars, who do you think of first?"

Rarely would consumers say Mitsubishi or any of its subbrands. This is called top-of-mind awareness. Furthermore, when interviews would probe along the lines of what other cars came to mind, Mitsubishi and its line of cars were mentioned far less often than most other major car manufacturers.

A lack of bonding was evident as Mitsubishi owners were seen to be less likely to cite their own cars than owners of other types of cars when asked what car they think of first. Bonding is one of those esoteric things that different research companies have different ways of quantifying. The graphic representation is usually in the shape of a pyramid. The base is how many people are familiar with your brand. The next level is relevance. You may be familiar with Aames Home Loan, but if you don't own a home or plan to in the immediate future, the brand has no relevance to your needs. The next level is advantage. Do consumers see an advantage or purpose in your brand for themselves? At the top is bonding, the number of consumers who plan on shopping for your brand. Mitsubishi's pyramid got too skinny too quickly.

Mitsubishi pickup trucks had a much healthier pyramid, but we at Deutsch were charged with increasing car sales. One strategy could have been to tell Mitsubishi that it wasn't a car manufacturer. That wasn't the answer they were looking for. There wasn't much appealing within Mitsubishi's heritage. It had recently been sued for environmental misgivings and sexual discrimination. If you looked back far enough, you could see that the company arose from an aircraft manufacturing company that made the planes that killed thousands of Americans at Pearl Harbor, hardly the fodder for endearment.

When a brand is healthy, looking for a larger imagistic space is a

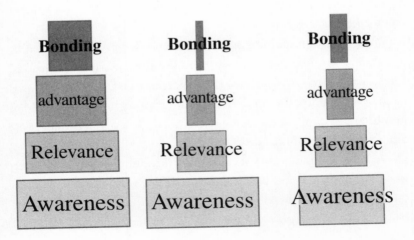

carefully plotted job. Mitsubishi was losing money quickly. It needed a space, any space, to give it some sales so it could catch its breath.

Target Analysis

- Current target.

- Competitive targets.

- Possible alternative targets.

- Relevance/contemporariness to current target/alternative targets: logos, fonts, colors, jingles, slogans/taglines, brand names, and other symbols.

- Unmet needs of target/alternative targets.

- Current consumer trends.

Purchasers of new Mitsubishi cars had appreciated the cars' style. A secondary comment was that these buyers liked a car that not everybody else has. We speculated that the combination of these two reported perceptions had led G2 to its "distinctive" positioning.

At Deutsch, we gave less credence to the second point of buyers preferring a car that not everybody else has. Experience suggested that few people actually enjoy owning a large-ticket item that isn't popular. The vast majority of these buyers had bought a Mitsubishi while they were actually shopping for other cars. These buyers had been test-driving cars on their consideration list and stumbled across a deal or financing for Mitsubishi that they couldn't find anyplace else. We drew an insight from this fact that Mitsubishi buyers were stretching financially to make their purchases. These were buyers who could more easily afford less expensive cars, but these less expensive cars felt staid when they were test-driven. Buying a Mitsubishi might be extending themselves, but they were getting the class of car that made them feel good. **To these buyers, the type of car they were buying was aspirational; we just needed to validate their choice.** Creating Mitsubishi to stand for vitality helped make that choice even easier. Can you see how this choice is not as easy if Mitsubishi stands for distinctive? Distinctive has overtures of staid—albeit classy staid, it is still low-testosterone.

Product Analysis

- Pricing: our brand vs. competitive landscape.
- Perceived quality: our brand vs. competitive landscape.
- Perceived value: our brand vs. competitive landscape.
- Points of parity with competition.
- Strengths: our brand vs. competitive landscape.

Mitsubishi didn't have a minivan. It was the only major manufacturer without a minivan and minivans had already crested in their popularity and were emblematic of family and everything nonvirile. Our first ads harangued minivan owners.

Messaging Analysis

- Assessment of equities: logos, fonts, colors, jingles, slogans/taglines, brand names, and other symbols.
- Messaging: our brand vs. competitive landscape.
- Packaging: our brand vs. competitive landscape.

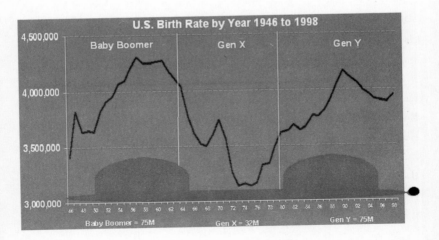

Another piece of data we were looking at was the pig in the python metaphor. If you graph the general population by age, it used to look like a python that swallowed a pig. Baby boomers create the hump. However, this metaphor is dated because the baby boomers had kids of their own. This generation is often called the echo boom generation or Generation Y. Whichever label you prefer, these young-sters are a second blip and are represented by the second hump. In 1998, there was no Ford Focus, no new VW; nobody was speaking to the emerging youth market. Vitality was perceived as having strengths against this emerging target.

Operational Analysis

- Possible alternative methods of distribution.
- Possible alternative packaging.
- Possible alternative pricing.

Mitsubishi had its own financing. This had more of an impact on amplification than it did on generating a brand essence. In amplification we'll discuss how this was valuable.

You aren't delving into these areas of consideration for due diligence. You are exploring these topics because they may be relevant for extracting your brand essence. And **your brand essence needs to be something that will help you make more money.**

That's a lot of work I just set out for you to do. You don't have to do it all. I'm just laying out the kind of preparation that goes into a brand strategy offsite. Please allow me to simplify this process for you.

Enough about you. How about me?

After having been disillusioned with big agency advertising, and not wanting to return to the hustle of a creative boutique, I ventured back out into freelancing—but with a much stronger focus on my writing, my fiction writing. I still freelanced in marketing, but I had to take a shot at becoming a famous novelist.

The Bucky Challenge

I will pay you $23 if you don't see The Matrix for 30 days-- Offer ONLY valid until 10/23/05...

Here's the deal...**If you read Poker Without Cards from beginning to end and don't see The Matrix for 30 days, I will mail you $23.** This is not a gag. There isn't an image of "The Matrix" in my book. I do reference the movie twice, but that's not this deal. The only trick is that by "The Matrix" I'm not talking about the movie The Matrix...

--I'm talking about seeing THE *MATRIX*, seeing a new REALITY! Usually this secret knowledge is abused to start cults or control the masses, but I explain how It works. If reading Poker Without Cards doesn't fundamentally alter the way you see the world I'll pay you $23 for wasting your time.

Do you want to break free from mass persuasion? I have the right credentials to teach you:
A) Magician--Magic Castle award winning magician; graduate of The Academy of Magical Arts' Junior Society, a real Hogwarts where Dai Vernon, David Copperfield & Lorenzo Clark tutored us kids
B) Ad Executive--Senior Vice President, Director of Brand Strategy for two large ad agencies
C) Realist--Tutored by Buckminster Fuller, Howard Bloom, Mike Caro, Jay Levinson & Dr. Hyatt
D) Hustler/Salesman--e.g., I sold over $22k of pizza in 3 days at Bonnaroo Music & Art Festival '05

I suck at designing my own ad. My friend J.W. @ ARNOLD emailed: "ben: i sayeth unto you: get thee to an art director. my head almost exploded with the *dizzying* array of font sizes and colors." I'm sorry this ad isn't better. I wasn't the guy that got paid to make the doughnuts at ad agencies. But this main message is so simple I'm making this ad...If you read Poker Without Cards and you think that I owe you $23 I'm sending it to you, one question asked. *If you can say "yes" I will pay you $23.*

I ask one question: Did poker without cards not work for you? You write me, "Yes, Poker without Cards didn't work for me and I read every word on every page." And I send you $23. All you have to do is mail me a Self-Addressed-Stamped-Envelope[SASE] and I will send you a money order for $23. Please don't be an asshole.

Clearly Channeling just for profits SUCKS.

I trust you. I trust you don't come to me with the intention of scamming me. Please don't scam me. You're a decent person. You read Arthur Magazine--I'm a struggling author pulling a stunt I hope you talk about--more than that **I want you to read my book.**

Its as easy as 1, 2, 3.
1) You read the book--You see THE *MATRIX* and feel satisfied and tell a friend, or:
2) You send me an email (email addy at book website: www.PokerWithoutCards.com) telling me you've finished the book and your not seeing THE MATRIX, your not seeing It
3) 30 days later you send me a *SASE* and I send you a money order for $23

Can't afford the book? About 200,000 were downloaded for free--ask them. But, I'm running out of cigarettes. So, now a download is $3.23. Read it by 9/23 and if it doesn't work for you I will send you $23. THIS IS A DIFFICULT BOOK. I transcribed the most powerful conversation I ever heard and put it in this book. To make the ideas more accessible, I added a glossary. I have done everything I know how to make these ideas as simple as possible and it is still a difficult book. If the word esoteric scares you please don't take my challenge. If the The Da Vinci Code is a thriller, Poker Without Cards is a consciousness fuck. Buy from the Independent store that gives you Arthur Magazine!

Thank you for your consideration.

Sincerely,

Benjamin Garth Siddhartha Mack
Sorry for the fake sig--I made this ad in PowerPoint

Ben Mack
p.s. Thank you STICK And MOVE for buying me this space! Reader, Please know they didn't write this clunky ugly ad. They make really good ads. Really. Two ex-Crispin creatives, of course they do!
p.p.s. Special Thanks to Michael Meaney and b. c. hydomako of RINF.com for my first online feature article. Order my book and **you will sleep better tonight, guaranteed!** Now, PokerWithoutCards.com

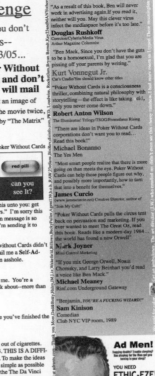

"As a result of this book, Ben will never work in advertising again. If you read it, neither will you. May this clever virus infect the mediaspace before it's too late."
Douglas Rushkoff
Coercion/Cyberia/Media Virus
Arthur Magazine Columnist

"Ben Mack, Since you don't have the guts to be a homosexual, I'm glad that you are pissing off your parents by writing."
Kurt Vonnegut Jr.
Cat's Cradle/You should know other titles

"Poker Without Cards is a consciousness thriller, combining natural philosophy with storytelling--the effect is like taking cid, only you never come down."
Robert Anton Wilson
The Illuminatus! Trilogy/TSOG/Prometheus Rising

"There are ideas in Poker Without Cards corportions don't want you to read... Read this book!"
Michael Bonanno
The Yes Men

"Most smart people realize that there is more going on than meets the eye. Poker Without Cards can help those people figure out why, and possibly more importantly, how to turn that into a benefit for themselves."
James Curcio
(www.jamescurcio.net) Creative Director, author of "Join My Cult!"

"Poker Without Cards pulls the circus tent back on persuasion and marketing. If you ever wanted to meet The Great Oz, read this book. Reads like a modern day 1984... the world has found a new Orwell"
Mark Joyner
Mind Control Marketing

"If you mix George Orwell, Noam Chomsky, and Larry Beinhart you'd read a voice like Ben Mack."
Michael Meaney
Rinf.com Underground Gateway

"Benjamin, *YOU'RE A FUCKING WIZARD!*"
Sam Kinison
Comedian
Club NYC VIP room, 1989

Ad Men!
laughing cheaply? Trouble sleeping? Not sleeping for the illest pay you trying to your sleep?
YOU NEED ETHIC-EZE!
FAST ACTING RELIEF FOR YOUR TROUBLED CONSCIENCE

Recommended by 4 out of 5 paranoias.

Bob Larbel of Portland, Oregon writes "Feelings of remorse nearly ruined my career at Sasquatch & Seaquatch. But now I'm proud of the work I on Ethic-Eze made sleeping pounds of guilt seemed effortless. Thank you."

In 2005 I tried selling righteousness in the form of a consciousness thriller. Consensus reality is wrong; here's truth. Truth is a tough sell unless you're willing to be a religious leader or at least a guru. And societies eventually reject their gurus. I like money more than I like being right. I garnered a lot of attention but I didn't make any money on the book. Have you Googled me?

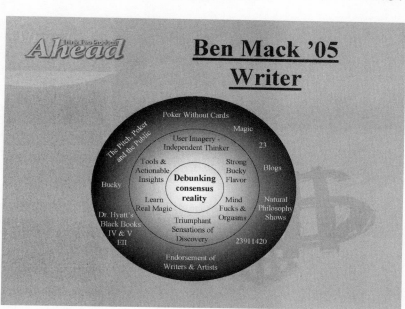

You'll find a lot of links. I created an online splash with a book called *Poker Without Cards*. See the Mack '05 Legend Platform I worked from.

How is my reader the hero? Because my readers have mental breakthroughs most people don't have.

Last year I focused on promoting my first novel. Now I'm focusing on freelancing, lecturing, and writing. Some of my associations weren't productive. My public connection to 23rdians made some people see me as a wing nut. So, I've distanced myself from those forums, even though I still read a lot of that literature. I love wing nuts—happy, successful wing nuts.

But, as you look at my revised Legend Platform you'll see the same brand essence and many similar product benefits.

Evolve your props, or your brand promise

not your brand essence, if possible.

Dear Reader,

I am sincerely grateful for the time you have spent with my words. If you have found value here and wish to share this value with your friends, my name is Ben Mack. If you found my ideas boring, trite, or offensive, my name is David Copperfield.

Let me ask for the sale. If you found value here, please tell your friends as you give them a copy of *Think Two Products Ahead*. Invite them to my Direct Response Branding Boot Camp.

Please document the changes you make based on this material and track changes in sales. I'll post your case studies at www.Think TwoSalesAhead.com. Thank you for your consideration.

I am a magician. I've been interested in performing magic since I was four years old. My essence hasn't changed. I'm still debunking reality, but instead of levitating a ball onstage, I show people magic tricks of the mind. My goal has always been to show business folks how looking at something differently can be profitable.

Thank you in advance for sharing your story.

With gracious gratitude,

Ben Mack

P.S. Here's a quote I admire: "We are what we repeatedly do. Excellence, then, is not an act, but a habit."—Aristotle

P.P.S. The most appropriate and famous last words I could find: "How were the receipts today at Madison Square Garden?"—P.T. Barnum. He said those words and died.

P.P.P.S. The best last words I've ever heard were from my friend Susan Carter's aunt, who said, "I'd like to be someplace better." And she closed her eyes forever. Did she plan that?

P.P.P.P.S. Would you like to see the most amazing card trick you'll ever see in your entire life? Hire me for a presentation. I do magic. Contact me at BenMackResearch@gmail.com.

B

Jeff Lloyd's Secret to Commercial Residential Real Estate Sales

Dear Reader,

You're still reading . . . hmmm. Okay, time to get to the marrow of making money. I warned you that you read the appendix at your own risk. What follows is not for the squeamish. However, if you are interested in how a 14-year-old runaway became a multimillionaire and what he is generous enough to share with me, then keep reading. But first, allow me to introduce Jeff Lloyd of Horizon Realty in West Hollywood, California. If you give him a call, tell him I sent you. Thank you for your consideration.

I met Jeff Lloyd sitting across from me at a seven-card-stud table at Commerce Casino in Los Angeles. I was arguably a rising star in consumer research and Jeff was struggling financially, having trouble scraping together alimony and owning zero real estate. Ten years later, Jeff owns over 40 commercial residential buildings outright, and if I include his various partnerships, where he owns more than 25 percent, over 100 buildings.

Jeff is not the richest man in Los Angeles, obviously. He is surely not even the wealthiest man on his block. So, why is he remarkable? He's Jeff Lloyd. Is that a copout? Yes. But it's also true.

Jeff is a proverbial Horatio Alger story, orphan turned millionaire. True to form, if you want to see him get angry, show him that you feel sorry for him. If you want to see him get really angry, try disrespecting a stripper. But, I suggest you be prepared to fight. Jeff has been successfully working on his anger management, but interacting with a volatile soul can be dangerous to your health, a lesson Jeff's brother Joby helped teach me.

Barring Buckminster Fuller and possibly Charles Munger, Jeff Lloyd is the smartest man with whom I have had the privilege of extended conversations. Jeff is autodidactic, having taught himself what the streets and mentors didn't teach him. His perspectives are shaped more from experience and internal judgment than from external forces or schools of thought. Jeff has made his own money and is beholden to no one. To these ends, more than anyone I have otherwise known, Jeff is his own man.

Jeff is a pirate of exquisite mind, a philanthropist, and a loving father.

I've been tempted to exploit pirate imagery and associated homonyms. For instance, it is easy for my mind to link sails and sales because both are instruments that harness energy. I have chosen to spare you. More accurately, I have chosen to spare myself the ridicule employing such imagery would warrant.

Pirates of yesteryear had comprehensive skills, knowledge required to live outside the system. The only laws that could, and did, rule them were natural laws. Pirates battled with one another to see who was going to control the vast sea routes and, eventually, the world. The wider and more long-distanced their anticipatory strat-

egy, the more successful they usually were. Their battles took place out of sight of land dwellers and the keepers of written history. The losers generally went to the bottom of the sea. Those who stayed on top of the waters and prospered did so because of their comprehensive abilities.

Salespeople can be seen as corporate pirates. They live outside the normal rules of companies, they create their own structure, and they are rewarded in direct proportion to their comprehensive abilities. But corporate salespeople are more like privateers, sanctioned to find bounty along specific sea routes and given a modicum of support from a larger organization.

Jeff Lloyd is a real pirate, making money however he can, taking personal responsibility for the sailors he has taken about his ship. His strongest defense is his greatest asset, an exquisite mind. But, be warned, this book swims in shark-infested waters. We speak pirate here, not "Arrr" or whatever gobbledygook you've seen in movies, but with words like *shit* and *fuck* and the vernacular of the street and the Street. I've been a senior vice president for two large ad agencies, I've hung with some C-level players of Fortune 1,000 companies, and they say *fuck* a lot. Not many business books use the word *fuck*. How real is that?

Jeff Lloyd is a philanthropist. Yes, his company is a corporate sponsor of The Covenant House, but that donation was made with a mixture of love and spite. He has deep love and empathy for homeless teenagers, but a major force in his donation was to show local business folks that if somebody like him can afford to pony up, so should they. Giving money in this way doesn't make somebody a philanthropist. Consistently, I see Jeff teaching others how to pull themselves up by their bootstraps. He's willing to be financially burned or personally disappointed by any given person. He doesn't care. Jeff knows that some folks will make use of what he can offer and that possibility lights him up. I hold that this makes him a philanthropist.

When I told Jeff about my work with Jay Levinson, how Jay teaches small business owners to harness the marketing techniques of big business advertising, his eyes lit up. That conversation led to this book. He wanted to teach others what he has learned about selling. He has a real estate brokerage where he teaches his agents how to sell, but that isn't fulfilling to him. From what I've seen, most of them are lazy. It is hard to stay motivated when a half-ass effort is netting $200,000 a year. That's why Jeff suggests choosing a wife who inspires you to make more money.

That is Jeff Lloyd's first tip: *Choose a wife who will inspire you to make money.*

I would be remiss if I ignored the role of Jeff's ego in commissioning me to write his biography, a project that has stalled. I fit Jeff's criteria of a man with a dream and I have never screwed him. But, what really lit him up was the opportunity to have his tale well told. I hope I hold up my end of this deal, and if his biography comes to pass I hope it will allow a few people to glimpse his grandeur and the means to his success. Jeff thinks he has led an extraordinary life. I hold this as undeniable. Jeff's ego is not to be discounted. He is a brave man for allowing me to write candidly about my observations.

There are many elements of this book that a critic can use as fodder for ridicule. I explained to Jeff that this part of *Think Two Products Ahead*, his story, might be described as ridiculous, literally worthy of ridicule. Jeff replied: "That's the price of being extraordinary. Many people describe me as ridiculous."

Jeff is a loving father. I hold that Jeff is a good father. Jeff once beat the shit out of his oldest son Brandon and says that if he were in a similar position he would do it again. Having been raised by a pacifist father, a man who spanked me only once when I tried to hit my sister with a rake when I was four, listening to Jeff speak about parenting I was confronted with a parenting style that I had never considered. I found that once I got over my shock and prejudices I saw warmth and effectiveness. I'm still judgmental. I think beating your son to the point of needing emergency care is excessive, bordering on wrong. However, if I was forced to say good dad or bad dad, I'd say Jeff is a good dad and Brandon agrees.

Traveling with Jeff was mind expanding. I was repeatedly discomfited or pleasured in unexpected ways. I was often disoriented, not just from drinking, but from confronting my own values—from abandoning pride as Jeff bought me my first hooker to feeling extraordinarily vulnerable as Jeff's friend insinuated I could have some portion of $120,000 cash if I would give this friend a blow job, something I had never done before. Traveling with Jeff in Mexico, I got bloodied, I bought cocaine from a Tijuana cop, and I got my girl back. My ego is huge and I hope to temper my inclination to steal the spotlight. What follows is a brief encapsulation of lessons I learned while recording Jeff's life story. If we do complete his biography, you'll be horrified, captivated, impressed, and relieved to know things have worked out fairly well for this gentleman.

The lesson you are about to read is written from interviews that occurred on two road trips in 2005 that both originated from Los Angeles: one trip to Nowhere, Arizona, to see whether Jeff wanted to evict a past-due tenant and the other to Ensenada, Mexico, where Jeff was racing in the Baja 500. I'm not a fan of off-road racing.

During our conversation Jeff was concerned about whether his story would be appealing. I assured him it was. Everybody is fascinated by money. The fastest-growing sport on ESPN is poker—you get rid of those cumbersome balls and vast open fields and you just televise people competing for money. Even if you aren't interested in Nicole Kidman inviting Jeff up to her hotel room and then kicking him out, at least you might pick up a trick or two about making *more* money.

I intersperse Jeff Lloyd's quotes with my commentary. I hope you dig this. I'm calling this essay . . .

Get the Shit Out

Jeff: I'm a salesman. Salespeople make more money than anybody. Isn't that the case?

I disagree with Jeff. Billionaires make more money than anybody else. But, next to those who are already independently wealthy, salespeople make more money than anybody else. Jeff didn't hear me say this. When the type is not italicized, it's me commenting. When I've transcribed Jeff's and my conversation, it looks like this:

> *Ben:* There's a lot of people out there who pride themselves on working really hard and don't have much to show for it.
>
> *Jeff:* Yeah, that's true. Well, I guess I'm lucky then. *(Laughs.)* Right?
>
> *Ben:* Well, I think you also chose something where you can make larger amounts of money and stuff like that.
>
> *Jeff:* Yeah, you always avoided coming over to the company even though I've asked you a bunch of times. . . . Nobody in my office makes less than 100 grand a year. And let me tell you, they're not that bright and they're not that dedicated. I can tell you exactly how to make a quarter mil a year.

Jeff's path to making $250,000 involves selling real estate. Obviously, you need a real estate license. You also have to have a desire to make a lot of money. Jeff makes the point that salesmen make the most money, but he's not speaking about all salesmen. The guy at Sears selling vacuum cleaners isn't making very much. Salesmen selling big-ticket items make the most amount of money. Few things cost more than developed real estate. The trick is not just selling real estate, but selling expensive real estate.

> *Jeff:* I saw that it took as much to sell a house as it did to sell a four-unit apartment building. But I was wrong. It often takes more time and energy to sell a small house than it does to sell commercial [residential] because a small buyer is scared of any substantial transaction because either they haven't done it before or because it means so much more to them. Also, you want to sell businesses instead of homes. Commercial residential may be

where people live, but the buyers are buying a business. When somebody buys their own home they move slowly. When somebody buys an income stream they generally move faster, especially after they have done this four or five times.

Velocity and commission. Allow me to elaborate: It's all-around more efficient to sell big-ticket items. Here's why: If you make 6 percent commission on a transaction, not only does it take eight $250,000 home sales to equal one $2 million commercial residential sale, but the residential sale may take longer and require more hand-holding of the buyer. I challenged this notion. I asked about our friend Danny Scott, a legendary car salesman. Danny nets over $350,000 year working the desk of a car dealership in Southern California.

Jeff: If Danny worked for me he'd be netting over a million in less than two years. Danny knows how to sell, but he's wasting his skills nickel-and-diming folks over a thousand dollars here and there. He's in a place where the customers come to him and so his skills are maximized in terms of quantity [of transactions]. But if he splits a $10 million commission he's made $300 grand. Danny could do that.

Confidence. It's all about the confidence. Jeff has a confidence that appears unshakable. It *is* unshakable. I've seen Jeff explode in anger, but I've never seen Jeff lose his stride. Jeff explained to me that he avoids things that make his sphincter squeeze up. He said that simply noticing this is a key to sustainable confidence and increased effectiveness. You can't have confidence and be full of it.

Jeff: I never cared about having a good car. It didn't make any difference to me. Up until 1996 I was driving a Ford Probe and before that I drove Toyotas. I had a Toyota 4-Runner, some Celicas—I mean, in reality, kids' cars—but I didn't see it that way. You know, I didn't care, because I liked the fact it was 8,000 bucks for the Probe or the 15,000 for the 4-Runner—no money at all, really, when you get down to the scheme of things for somebody making hundreds of thousands of dollars. But I remember I went to a client's house, a good client of mine. It made no difference what car I was driving—they were doing the deal with me. But they walked out with me and saw my Ford Probe and the lady client said, "Oh, isn't this what the kids drive?" and my sphincter tightened *(Laughs.)* or whatever you wanna say, and I said, "Um, yeah, I like it because it's cheap." That just didn't sound right. It did not work in sales. And I said, well, Jeff, I guess you gotta man up and go buy a car because you can't have your clients thinking that you're a kid or less of you because you don't drive a real car. And I thought it was shallow and I wanted to rage against the machine *(Laughing.)*, you know, but why? Rage against the machine all you want on your own time. When you're selling properties and you're doing sales you go with the machine because the machine is what's making the money. So I bought myself a BMW right after that and immediately my sales became easier. People questioned me so much less. It was like a phenomenon. All of a sudden I had instant respect because I drove a BMW. *(Laughs.)* I mean I was shocked. I didn't know. Nobody ever told me these things, you know. How would I have known?

So, the car you drive affects your sales efforts. Nobody told Jeff straight up. He didn't have a business mentor or parent. Much of what is covered in this book is what he wished somebody had told him. In another tip, I'll cover Jeff elaborating on how and why your car is so important to your confidence. Sustainable confidence comes from nurturing your confidence. Nurturing your confidence starts with noticing when your confidence is waning, to notice your *sphincter*. If you feel your sphincter tightening, notice this and find a way to take action. You don't want to be constipated.

Jeff explained that he noticed his sphincter tighten when he didn't know something about his profession. As opposed to ignoring what he didn't know, which he sees many people going way out of their way to do, he'd go study the crap out of the subject.

> *Jeff:* What I did was work really, really hard. When you're the owner of the company, believe me, you're not sitting on easy street. You're working harder than anybody else when you're the owner. The idea of the fat corporate cat? I think that's a poor guy's mantra.
>
> I've seen that actually where a poor guy gets in charge or something and he sticks his feet up on the desk and he is quickly relieved of all that responsibility. (Jeff laughs, meaning the business goes away, goes bankrupt.) You know, [poor folks] want to get there so they don't have to work. Please. Let me say to all you poor people out there: You're not working near as much as the rich people are, so unless you're talking about old money filthy rich, the rich are working really hard.

If I told you the secret to being a millionaire salesperson was hard work, you'd laugh at me. Hard work isn't a secret—it's a table stake. Jeff pounds this point. You can skip this next bit if you are already a seven-figure salesperson. There's a lot of hard work to making a lot of money. But, Jeff off-handedly commented to me that the seven-figure salespeople often review the basics. He finds an openness and humility in very successful salespeople that he doesn't see in most other folks.

> *Jeff:* I see really successful sellers learning and working. It is how they get better than the less successful—learning, learning, learning, learning, working, working, working, working.

The harder I work, the luckier I get and the less I have to do later. So my suggestion to all you readers out there is that if you start young, work extremely hard when you're young, because as you get older you really don't feel like it. *(Laughs.)* So stop thinking, "This is my life, I gotta enjoy myself." Because you're full of shit. Because as you get older you really won't feel like it is your life if you don't work hard when you're young. You know how many young people, young kids these days *(Laughs.)*, they say, "I'm not gonna do that!" You know, they're too good for it. They leave at five o'clock, because that's quitting time. That's great, if you're working at 7-Eleven and you're very comfortable with your life, and you like going to your apartment and turning on your 19-inch TV and what have you.

But if you're a self-employed person—you know, I really never work less than half days, you know, nine to nine. *(Laughs.)* So there's no set time frame in real estate or what have you. You have to work and work and work.

People who don't work hard or don't work smart see me as lucky.

When I started out in real estate I used to work from seven to midnight. I got a call one time at midnight. This guy had a property down in Wilmington. John Cleburne was his name, and the phone rings at midnight and I'm at Fred Sands realtors. This is 1988 and I answered the phone and he said, "Wow, I was just gonna leave a message." And I said, "Well, I'm here. What do you need?" He said, "Well, I have a property on King Street down in Wilmington that I want to sell. It's a four-plex and I needed to know what it was worth." I said, "Well, I'm a broker," and I took down the information and then I sold him a property in Sol Mar. So, I guess I was just lucky, wasn't I, to be there at midnight? *(Laughs.)* The harder I work the luckier I get. *(Laughs.)* The problem with that theory, though, is that for seven years I worked every day every moment, *(Sings.)* "Every breath you take, every move you make." I didn't do anything but work. People would say to me, "Jeff, you know, there are other things to talk about than work." Nobody really wanted to hang around me because all I did was talk about work. I was so enamored and so in love with real estate and success after having been a homeless street kid with no high school education that I didn't do anything but work.

When I met my second wife for the first time she looked into my closet. I was still married to my first wife, but Christine was living Colorado at that time and I was closing on my company and I was working really hard. She opened up my closet and all there were were suits except for one pair of pink shorts in that closet that were my brother-in-law Mark's that I inherited when he died. They were the only casual clothes that I owned. I owned nothing else but suits. And I hadn't realized that. I was shocked when she told me that. And I thought about it and I went wow. I said I'd better go buy a pair of jeans. And it kinda just changed right then and there. And I took a year off of work and went snowboarding and fishing in 1994, the whole year. I didn't work at all to speak of. And I learned. I remember sitting in my motor home on Thanksgiving Day, cooking my turkey, looking out at the slope of Breckenridge and just feeling really good.

The image I had in my mind as Jeff was telling me this was of a woman jogger, jogging with a golden retriever on a leash, a really happy golden retriever. The golden retriever had his leash in his mouth. Sure, he was on a leash, but he was out and jogging and while he was on a leash, he was carrying his own leash. That's the point I was hearing, that the secret to freedom was to carry your own leash.

Finding a balance is critical. When I met Jeff in 1995, a year after his yearlong vacation, he was almost bankrupt, perilously close to missing alimony payments. We'll get to more of that later. I wanted to understand how I can make my quarter million. How I can carry my own leash.

> *Ben:* What are some of the other secrets to sales success or success in selling? What would I need to know for me to make that quarter million you promised you could teach me earlier?

> *Jeff:* I've found it's easy to forget when teaching somebody the basics of sales because, when you're very successful and you make a lot of money like I do, you think it just came naturally. *(Laughs.)*
>
> But then I have to go ahead and think back and I realized that this is the way that I found out that I learned things. I forget what I learned.
>
> I know it's gonna sound kind of funny, but I was listening to Sam Kinison and I always thought Sam Kinison was the funniest guy alive. He's dead now, but I still think he was the funniest comedian ever. A lot of people won't agree with that and I really don't care, but I thought he was hilarious. And so, maybe five years went by and I hadn't really listened to him and I bought his CD and I listened to him and I realized that half my jokes that I say as part of my everyday repertoire were from Sam Kinison. *(Laughs.)* I mean, I yell over to one of my agents, "Hey, Scotty, can you come here and bring everything in your desk?" That's Sam Kinison, but I didn't remember that that was Sam Kinison.
>
> It's the same thing as salespeople. Yeah okay, some people are born salespeople—usually we call them shysters. *(Laughs.)* Other people are just regular people that like to sell and can talk to people or what have you, but it's not that natural a thing to be the perfect salesman, and so you learn. I wasn't a natural salesman.

And so the way you learn is you listen to the great sales-people. You listen to Tony Robbins and although I don't really like Tony Robbins that much (I don't like his bouncy attitude thing), let me tell you, when I'm sitting in my car, I've learned something from him that I do. If I'm feeling kind of lousy, I smile.

I know this is not me. This technique is from a sales tape or Anthony Hopkins or somebody else that I'd listen to one time or a book that I read. The act of smiling makes me feel better.

So therefore if I'm feeling lousy just before going into an appointment, I smile. Smile, smile, smile. I learned that. What I'm saying is that, through all of these training programs and techniques, "how to swim with sharks and not get eaten alive," "the one-minute salesperson," or, like I said, Tony Robbins, all these different salespeople, I picked up things from each of them and I learned. I learned a line from each one of them and I came to believe that it was all me. Well, I am a culmination of all the things that I've done.

Ben: But you called natural salespeople shysters.

Jeff: I've developed a sales technique that is the art of not selling and that's one that's working for me best right now. And I can tell you that, if the art of not selling anything is not working for me, I'll change it again. Change spurs growth, and anytime you change something you end up growing in some direction. If it's a bad direction, change it. Grow again in a different direction. So, everything you do, everything you learn, everything you read, everything you listen to, if you apply it in everyday sales, you'll find out if it works really quickly.

Like, for example, I heard the term "economy of scale" one time. I thought economy of scale—what the hell does economy of scale mean? I *(Laughs.)* really don't know what that means and so somebody told me that it meant there's more money to be made with less in some ways. So I said to myself, that's interesting. So [I was with a client and] we were walking through an apartment building and he said, "Geez, these units are really small." And I said, "Yeah, isn't that great?" Now, you might sit there and go, "Well, that's a stupid remark," and the guy goes, "Well, what do you mean?" And I said, "Well, the economy of scale is perfect here. People rent small units. A lot of people like small units. You know, smaller places to live, less to clean, but beyond the fact that it's very rentable is the fact that it is for you so much cheaper to carpet, so much cheaper to paint and to take care of because the economy of scale, because it's smaller and you get more rent per square foot and it costs you less in maintenance to run it. That's why I like small units." It just came out of my mouth, but since then I've used that line a lot, and I've never had anybody refute that. So, that's an interesting thing. I mean you can sell anything you want to sell as long as you don't sound like you're selling.

Now does that sound like selling to you? I don't think it does.

To answer Jeff's question now, yes, that sounds exactly like selling to me. I don't think that Jeff is practicing not selling. I see Jeff as learning to not come across as a shyster. I'm reminded of words by Larry Beinhart, author of *Wag the Dog*: "Propaganda that sounds like propaganda is second-rate propaganda." What I'm hearing Jeff say is that selling that sounds like selling is second-rate selling.

Jeff is at a stage in his career when he is beginning to sell really expensive properties and to navigate bigger sellers through more complicated deals. The bigger the deal, the less appropriate it is to sound like a salesperson.

I think what Jeff is demonstrating is that when you internalize knowledge it no longer feels awkward. When he feels lousy, he smiles. This has become second nature. It wasn't a natural instinct to smile when he felt lousy. But, through practicing techniques, you continue doing what is effective.

Improving salesmanship becomes the practice of adopting what is effective. Yes, it might not feel natural at first, but if something helps get the job done, you do it. You might have an inclination to rage against the machine, but if that is getting in the way of sales, then the professional salesperson puts these inclinations aside and does what will be more effective because that is what it means to be a professional. You're choosing your actions because you are attempting to make money.

If money is the goal, learn to sell, and learn to sell big-ticket items. Making money isn't about being comfortable while you're making money. Making money is about being comfortable later. Making money is about carrying your own leash or, better yet, being able to forget you've got a leash. Making money is about, well, making money.

> *Jeff:* You need to know your business. That's a given. You learn to see opportunities and bigger opportunities. Then the real trick is to navigate around the shit.

The biggest thing about making money is focusing on making money. Get rid of what is wasting your time to make more money.

> *Jeff:* When I'm fighting with my wife, I'm just not wanting to deal with the shit. Shit gets in the way of everything, having a life and making money. Drama is shit. Drama is unnecessary tension, tension is friction, and friction slows everything down.

Quibbling gets in the way of making money. The best way to make money is to make money quickly.

Jeff: The job of a finance person is not to tell me what I can't do. The job of a finance person is to tell me what they need to get the job done. I don't want to hear their shit. I want them to tell me they will get the financing. If they fuck up once I won't work with them again. I can't afford to.

Jeff explained that by keeping his name clean, clients are willing to move faster with him. And as he has progressed as a salesman he has evolved to work with folks who are willing to work quickly. It is more valuable to him to give up a commission than to quibble.

Jeff: I've had many situations where I said, "Take my commission. If you really feel that I didn't represent you, take it." Just last year, a client of mine said to me (I never liked this guy, first of all, but I've made a lot of money for him and with him), "Jeff, you didn't represent me." And I said, "Yes, I did." He said, "No, you didn't. Don't talk to me anymore. Talk to my attorney." I failed right there because I didn't spend enough time with this particular client that I knew needed a super amount of hand-holding and everything else, and in fact I had become too big for him. While I had made money by working with him, investing time with him now was costing me more than he was worth in potential revenue. It is assessing the opportunity and the opportunity cost that helps you make more money. I already knew who he was.

"What's the point of complaining?" my psychiatrist asked me when I said, "You know, my wife is doing this and she's doing that to me. I can't believe it." I'd tell the story of whatever she did, and I'd say, "I just can't believe it." And he said, "When are you gonna stop being amazed?" And I said, "What do you mean?" And he said, "You already know what she's doing to you. You know you keep going through the same kind of thing and yet you continue to be shocked."

It's the same thing with your clients. If you know who they are and you know they're assholes and you're still working with them, why are you complaining? Just learn how to deal with them. I've always said he who ends up with the commission in the end wins. Because you've sold it.

If people could get along they wouldn't need real estate brokers. *(Laughing.)* They wouldn't need salespeople or intermediaries. You are basically a filter for shit. *(Laughs.)*

I mean it's kind of an ugly statement, but you're a shit filter as a real estate broker. So you don't get anywhere with a client by telling them how bad the other person is because I'll tell you what, they'll stop wanting to work and cooperate. If you tell the buyer that the seller is an asshole, then the buyer is eventually gonna believe it and not want to be working with this guy. Then your job is doubly hard. So keep it in and filter it clean, you know.

Ben: That's your primary job as a salesman?

Jeff: Right, it really is. Filter the shit out.

How to Turn Every First Sale into a Residual Stream of Income

Direct Response Branding; FREE Seminar Details and Downloads

I'm Ben Mack.

You may have seen me on T. Harv Eker's World's Greatest Marketing Seminar. I'm better known in advertising for having created the yo-yo craze of 1998 where Yomega Yo Yos went from $8,000,000 a year to over $110,000,000.

I've been lead strategist on Publix and Cingular, among other national brands, but I prefer working with entrepreneurs and small businesses.

Tonight, I'm going to reveal to you...

Secrets the BIG ad agencies don't want you to know and how to use them for bigger profits...

Listen to the audio of this presentation Online, here...

http://www.**ThinkTwoProductsAhead**.com

You need a plan.

You need a communication plan that makes you more money than it costs. You need a brand. I don't mean a logo. Branding is the process of integrating all your messages for maximum profitability, where you are not only attracting all the customers you want but you are creating customers who want to do business with you again and again.

You need a communication plan that...

- Saves you time writing your copy.
- Turbocharges your communications by harnessing all your diverse messages into a focused voice.
- Identifies missing products and services that your customers need right now.
- Unifies your business team because everybody is literally on the same page.
- Makes your packaging and instructions build momentum toward your next sale.
- Invisibly integrates "next sale messaging."
- Directs your customers to see your products as a perfect fit for their needs.
- Boosts the effectiveness of direct response tactics.
- Creates the linger effect, where your messages linger in their minds.
- Teases, entices, and reinforces your marketing as customers user your products and services.
- Leverages your most profitable ideas harder, further, and faster.
- Never again wonder if an e-mail or ad is on strategy.
- Makes readers see how all your products and services are working together to help your customers achieve their goals and desires.
- Takes the guesswork out of writing your marketing.

Allow me to show you a communication plan...

http://www **ThinkTwoProductsAhead** .com

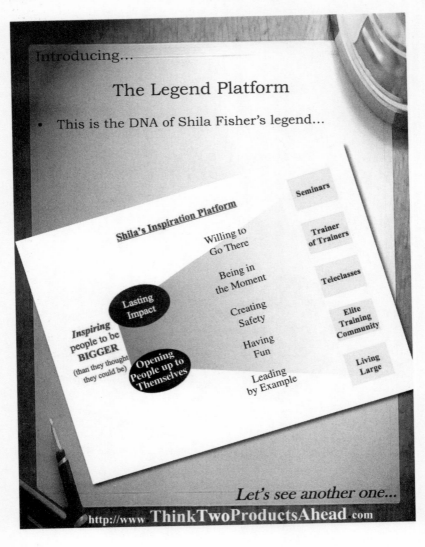

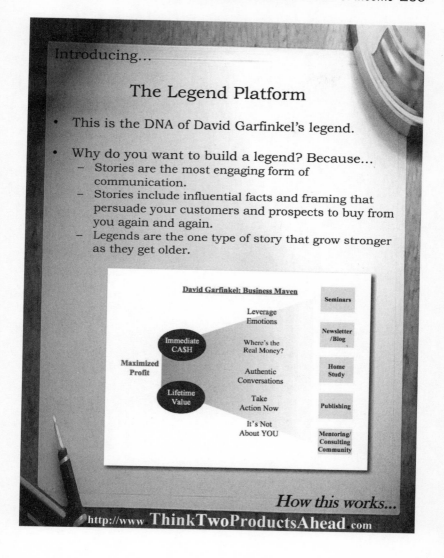

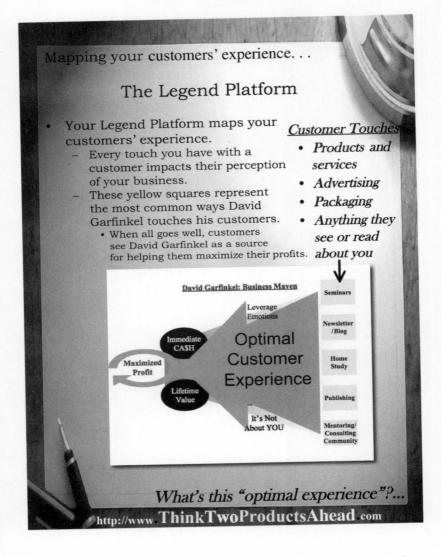

Mapping your customers' experience. . .

The Legend Platform

- Your Legend Platform maps your customers' experience.
    - Every touch you have with a customer impacts their perception of your business.
    - These yellow squares represent the most common ways David Garfinkel touches his customers.
        - When all goes well, customers see David Garfinkel as a source for helping them maximize their profits.

Customer Touches
- *Products and services*
- *Advertising*
- *Packaging*
- *Anything they see or read about you*

David Garfinkel: Business Maven

Leverage Emotions

Immediate CA$H

Maximized Profit

Lifetime Value

Optimal Customer Experience

It's Not About YOU

Seminars

Newsletter /Blog

Home Study

Publishing

Mentoring/ Consulting Community

What's this "optimal experience"?...

http://www.**ThinkTwoProductsAhead**.com

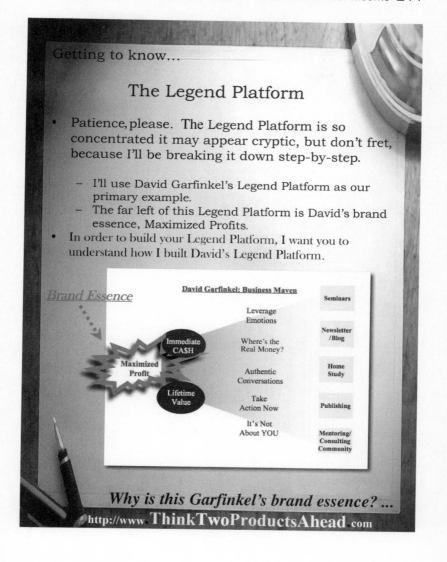

Getting to know...

The Legend Platform

- Patience, please. The Legend Platform is so concentrated it may appear cryptic, but don't fret, because I'll be breaking it down step-by-step.

  - I'll use David Garfinkel's Legend Platform as our primary example.
  - The far left of this Legend Platform is David's brand essence, Maximized Profits.
- In order to build your Legend Platform, I want you to understand how I built David's Legend Platform.

Why is this Garfinkel's brand essence? ...

http://www. **ThinkTwoProductsAhead** .com

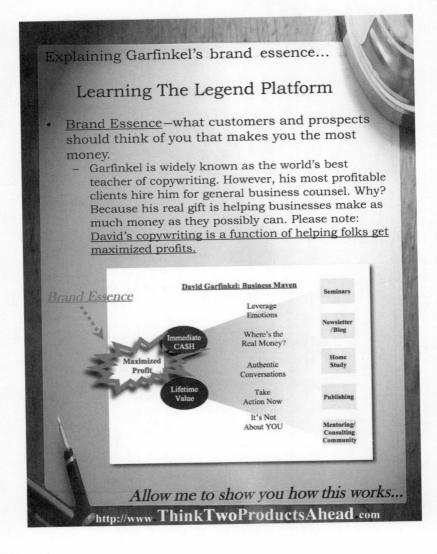

Explaining Garfinkel's brand essence...

Learning The Legend Platform

- <u>Brand Essence</u>—what customers and prospects should think of you that makes you the most money.
    - Garfinkel is widely known as the world's best teacher of copywriting. However, his most profitable clients hire him for general business counsel. Why? Because his real gift is helping businesses make as much money as they possibly can. Please note: <u>David's copywriting is a function of helping folks get maximized profits.</u>

Allow me to show you how this works...

We start REAL big...

Creating Your Legend Platform

Step 1

- Uncovering your brand essence:
    - What's the real benefit to your customer?
    - What's the big reason for people to give you money?
        - Intention here is to <u>Get the biggest benefit you can authentically service/deliver</u>.

Write your brand essence here...

Using your brand essence...

Building YOUR brand essence...

Using Your Legend Platform

- Every touch with your customers should build your brand essence.
    - You don't need to use the exact words of your brand essence.
    - Instead, use this sentence:

Does _____ reinforce (<u>my brand essence</u>)?

Before David Garfinkel writes his blog he asks himself...
Does <u>(this blog entry)</u> reinforce (<u>Maximized Profits</u>)?

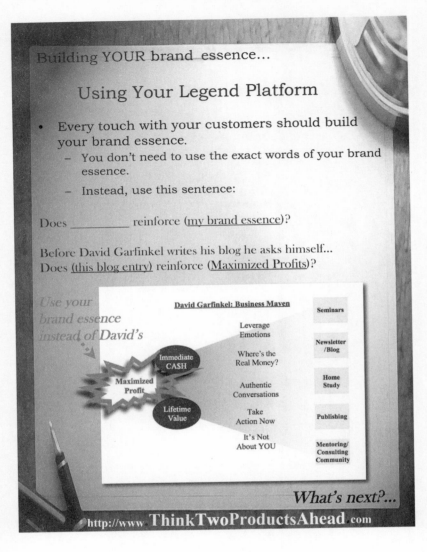

Use your brand essence instead of David's

David Garfinkel: Business Maven

Immediate CA$H

Maximized Profit

Lifetime Value

Leverage Emotions

Where's the Real Money?

Authentic Conversations

Take Action Now

It's Not About YOU

Seminars

Newsletter /Blog

Home Study

Publishing

Mentoring/ Consulting Community

What's next?...

http://www.**ThinkTwoProductsAhead**.com

You have active ingredients...

Learning The Legend Platform

- <u>Primary Principles</u> –Essential components that comprise your brand essence.
  - In order for Garfinkel to help clients or students maximize their profit, they must:
    - Generate as much immediate business as possible, getting as many new customers as possible.
    - Optimize for lifetime value of each customer, getting the most money from each of their existing customers as possible.

Garfinkel's Primary Principles

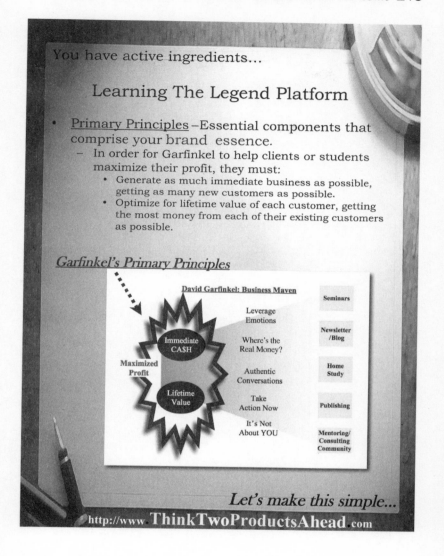

Let's make this simple...

http://www.**ThinkTwoProductsAhead**.com

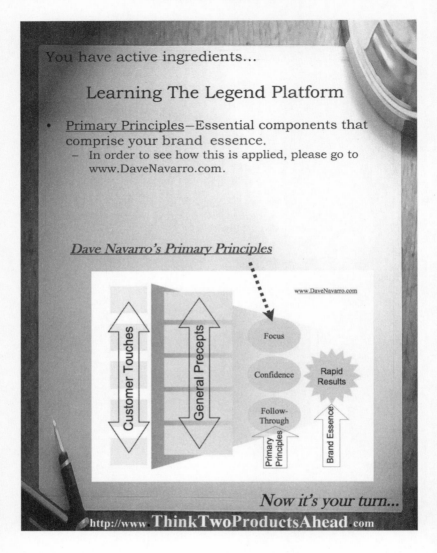

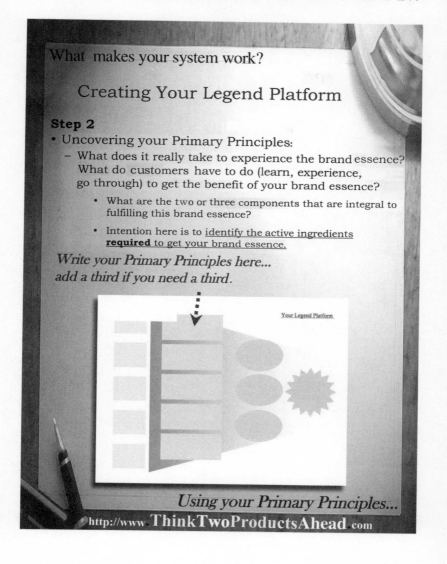

What makes your system work?

Creating Your Legend Platform

Step 2
- Uncovering your Primary Principles:
  - What does it really take to experience the brand essence? What do customers have to do (learn, experience, go through) to get the benefit of your brand essence?
    - What are the two or three components that are integral to fulfilling this brand essence?
    - Intention here is to <u>identify the active ingredients</u> **required** <u>to get your brand essence.</u>

Write your Primary Principles here...
add a third if you need a third.

Your Legend Platform

Using your Primary Principles...
http://www.**ThinkTwoProductsAhead**.com

Your Legend Platform

Using your Primary Principles builds your brand essence...

Using Your Legend Platform

- Writing or talking about your Primary Principles automatically builds your brand essence.
  - Since your Primary Principles are essential components of your Brand Essence, discussing these principles builds your brand essence. It's this easy.

Talking about how your products and services facilitate your Primary Principles gives customers the reason to believe they can experience your Brand Essence.

Discuss your Primary Principles frequently.

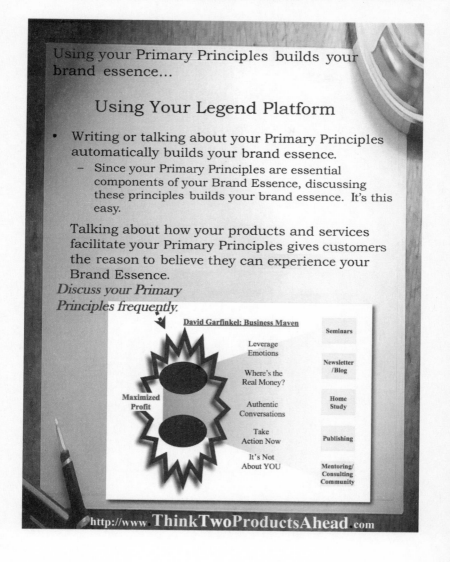

http://www.**ThinkTwoProductsAhead**.com

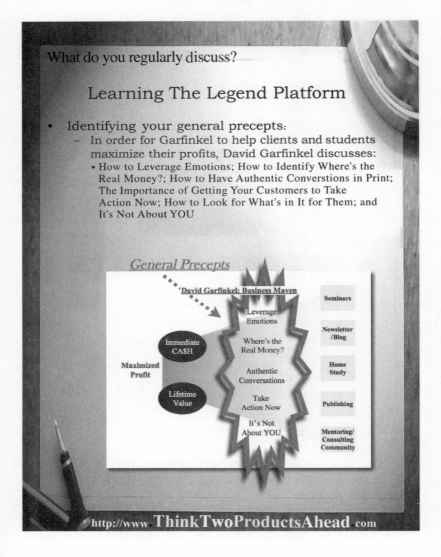

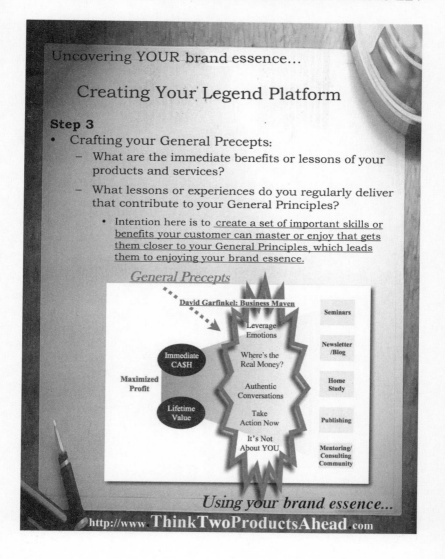

Uncovering YOUR brand essence...

Creating Your Legend Platform

Step 3

- Crafting your General Precepts:
  - What are the immediate benefits or lessons of your products and services?
  - What lessons or experiences do you regularly deliver that contribute to your General Principles?
    - Intention here is to <u>create a set of important skills or benefits your customer can master or enjoy that gets them closer to your General Principles, which leads them to enjoying your brand essence.</u>

General Precepts

David Garfinkel: Business Maven

Immediate CA$H

Lifetime Value

Maximized Profit

Leverage Emotions

Where's the Real Money?

Authentic Conversations

Take Action Now

It's Not About YOU

Seminars

Newsletter /Blog

Home Study

Publishing

Mentoring/ Consulting Community

Using your brand essence...

http://www.**ThinkTwoProductsAhead**.com

Building YOUR business...

Using Your Legend Platform

Step 4

- Do you have at least one product or service that teaches or provides a way for your customers to get these benefits?
    - For any General Precepts without a supporting product or service, you can create a new product that fits within your brand because this product fills a need for your customers to achieve your brand essence.
- Are you regularly addressing all of your General Precepts?
    - On your blog or through whatever regular contact you have with a customer you want to keep them familiar with ALL your precepts.

You now have a strong grasp of branding...

When you look at a possible ad, package, instruction...ask yourself:

Does _____ reinforce (my brand essence)?

- If the answer is "Yes," then you are building your brand.
- If the answer is "No," then consider how you can re-create the communication so you are building your brand essence.

http://www.**ThinkTwoProductsAhead**.com

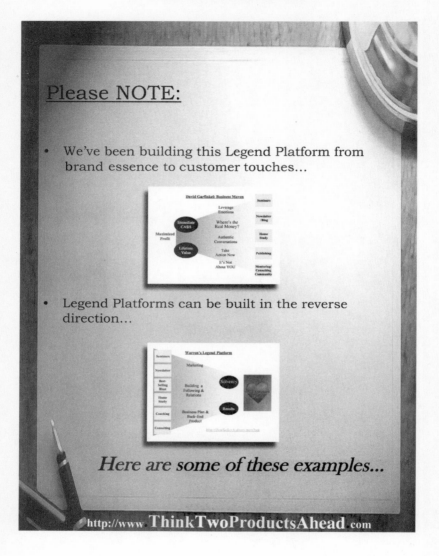

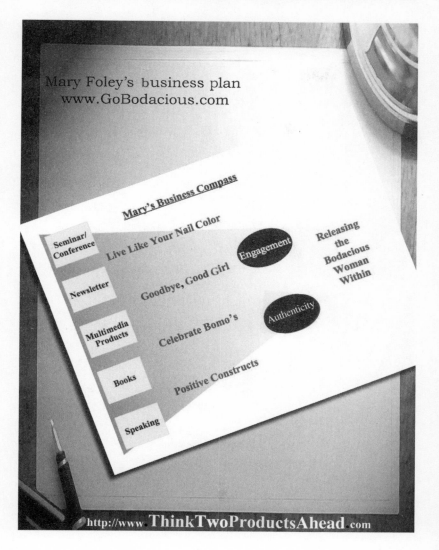

Mary Foley's business plan
www.GoBodacious.com

Mary's Business Compass

Seminar/Conference — Live Like Your Nail Color — Engagement — Releasing the Bodacious Woman Within

Newsletter — Goodbye, Good Girl

Multimedia Products — Celebrate Bomo's — Authenticity

Books — Positive Constructs

Speaking

http://www.ThinkTwoProductsAhead.com

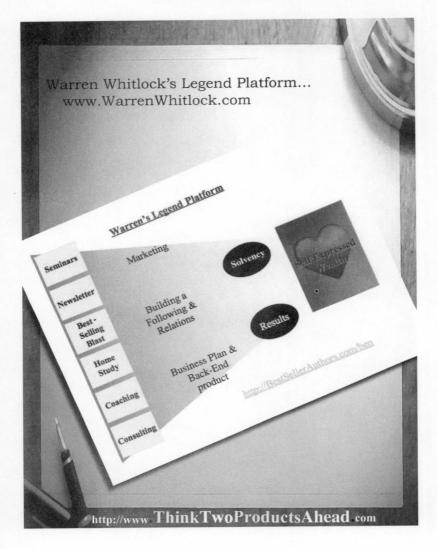

How to win all the customers you can handle and effortlessly keep them for life...

Don't settle for "this or that"!

Are you constantly breaking into a sweat with your marketing? If you've got loyal customers but have trouble getting more, *or* if you can get customers but they seem to wander away, this may be the most valuable Special Report you'll ever read.

You CAN'T make money without buyers...

Traditional **BRANDING** will ensure loyal customers, but some customers will always drift away.
- The problem is that you never really grow because you can't deliver new buyers when you need them.

Traditional **DIRECT RESPONSE** marketing will deliver buyers; however, they will be mostly one-off sales.
- The problem is that you never gain momentum when you are forced to constantly capture new customers.

The only thing that makes sense is...

Direct Response Branding.

http://www. **ThinkTwoProducts**Ahead .com

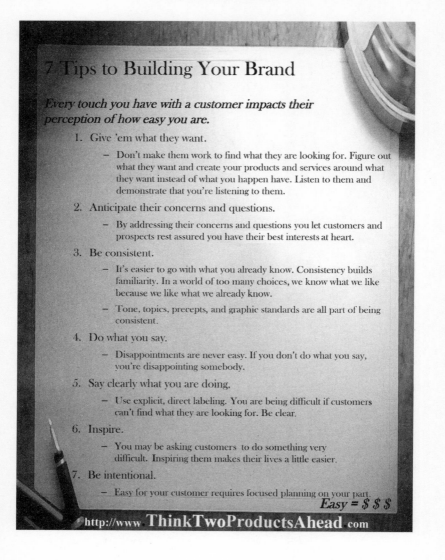

7 Tips to Building Your Brand

Every touch you have with a customer impacts their perception of how easy you are.

1. Give 'em what they want.
   - Don't make them work to find what they are looking for. Figure out what they want and create your products and services around what they want instead of what you happen have. Listen to them and demonstrate that you're listening to them.

2. Anticipate their concerns and questions.
   - By addressing their concerns and questions you let customers and prospects rest assured you have their best interests at heart.

3. Be consistent.
   - It's easier to go with what you already know. Consistency builds familiarity. In a world of too many choices, we know what we like because we like what we already know.
   - Tone, topics, precepts, and graphic standards are all part of being consistent.

4. Do what you say.
   - Disappointments are never easy. If you don't do what you say, you're disappointing somebody.

5. Say clearly what you are doing.
   - Use explicit, direct labeling. You are being difficult if customers can't find what they are looking for. Be clear.

6. Inspire.
   - You may be asking customers to do something very difficult. Inspiring them makes their lives a little easier.

7. Be intentional.
   - Easy for your customer requires focused planning on your part.

Easy = $ $ $

http://www. **ThinkTwoProductsAhead** .com

Your instructions and packaging should incite usage as effectively as your sales copy drove sales.

Design products and services that both exceed the buyer's expectations and entice a subsequent sale.

First, in order to exceed the buyer's expectations, you need to show the user how to get all the benefits you promised in your sales copy.

- When you explicity teach your customers to recognize their benefits and leverage these for personal gain, your products and services will make them happy by being easy to use.

Your customers will grow to enjoy your instructions because they are TRULY EXPERIENCING what's in it for them.

Second, after your customers have learned to trust that you give them what you promise, you explain how they can get even better benefits by buying another of your products or services.

- You show them their road map to the next level of enjoying your brand essence, something they can't get enough of.

http://www.ThinkTwoProductsAhead.com

This is a new concept in product and service development!

Direct response branding is marketing from the inside out.

All of your messaging needs to be built around your brand promise and your brand essence, leveraging the value of your precepts.

- Your messaging affects the experience of your product and your products and services impact the way customers engage with your messaging.

- Your headline drives traffic as it reflects your product's sustainable benefits (precepts).

- Your product delivers on your marketing promises and incites desire for more through its consumption and its packaging and instructions.

- You need direct response branding because you need products and services that are engineered to warm your customer to buy from you again and again and again and again.

http://www.ThinkTwoProductsAhead.com

What did we learn today?

You are twice as powerful a marketer as you think you are...

The real selling begins with their first purchase from you.
There is MAGIC right around the corner. No kidding. Once you begin combining the powerful persuasion of direct response with the charisma of branding, your sales will shoot up and your repeat business will explode.

Your biggest expense is getting a new customer.

- Most direct marketers create continuity haphazardly. Though their marketing is efficient, they leave a lot of money on the table by not thinking through continuity before they start.

Using **direct response** without **branding** is like having a car where the back tires and the front tires are going in opposite directions. You'll spend a lot of time, money, and energy and get nowhere!

- A simple direct response branding strategy, applied to series of consecutive marketing messages, not only makes money on every campaign, but increases profitability with every sale as it builds commands for repeat buying right into your products and services so *your current sales bring you sales tomorrow.*

http://www.**ThinkTwoProductsAhead**.com

$197 e-Book

Did you get $197 of value from Think Two Products Ahead?

The same book you've enjoyed reading was sold online for $197 as an e-book with a 98 percent buyer satisfaction.

The digital download of *Think Two Products Ahead* grossed $43,931.

Want to read the direct-response sales letter that not only sold the digital version of this book for $197 but ensured satisfaction of our buyers?

That's direct-response-branding. Please read the online sales letter at: www.ThinkTwoProductsAhead.com/Michael_Morgan.

Acknowledgments

This book is for all readers trying to scrape a better living for themselves. However, *Think Two Products Ahead* could not have reached this broad an audience without the bravery of my cutting-edge editor, Matt Holt.

If you are still reading this page you are probably hoping to see your name, so I'd like to apologize before I disappoint you. (I just ran out of space.)

The fact that you are holding the book in your hand must be attributed to Kim Dayman—not the Canadian artist with lingerie on her web site, but the Senior Marketer at John Wiley & Sons who stoked the flames of interest around this text. Matt and Kim, I owe you drinks.

Many thanks to my sister, Haley Mack, whose unconditional love and support are always with me. Haley has regularly helped me remember our parents' birthdays and forgiven me when I've forgotten hers.

I love you, Mom. And you well prepared me to intellectually engage with anybody. Before the age of 14 my mom had arranged for me to spend three days interviewing R. Buckminster Fuller and attend Anthony Robbins' Firewalk seminar and Bobbi Deporter's Super Camp.

To Dad and Betty, who demonstrated that ideals don't need to be compromised and that it is possible to never give up the dream of peace and love for all humanity—I love you.

Mark Joyner, Dave Lakhani, Kevin Hogan, Tellman Knudson, Sam Heyer, and Michael Morgan made this book possible by encouraging me. David Garfinkel for mentoring me.

T. Harv Eker for teaching me how to sell folks what they want and *then* give them what they need.

Larry Clark for teaching me magic, Joseph Matheny for teaching me magick, and Joe Grieco for teaching me to make money distinguishing the two.

Ah, making money. Gail Kingsbury, Karen Evans, Debbie Dupé, Sandra Love, and Dianna Zimmerman, who taught me to brand my magic.

Joel Bauer, who taught me to prospect from the stage.

Jeffrey Blish for teaching me strategy, Michael Sheldon for teaching me moxie, Eric Hirschberg for teaching me confidence, and Donny Deutsch for teaching me stature.

Weiner, Wong & Doody for hiring me as a memeticist and teaching me your game.

Ditto TG Madison. Arnie Fishman, Dave Sackman, David Froemke, and Brian McMahan for teaching me how to be a professional and the value of semantics.

Claire Furman for teaching me how to take a mental health day.

David Garfinkel for teaching me to sell from the page.

June Deery for teaching Media Literacy.

RPI colleagues for enduring my media ecology perspective.

Liz Crawford for teaching me how to take care.

Rich Wakefield, John Drake, Mike Delaune, Julie Foster, Susan Carter, Chris Titan, Fideliz Saroa, Amelia Smith, Shi Zhang, Harry Vardis, Gary Selden, Reshma Shah, Sara Hall, Cecelia Wogan, Philip Munger, and Joann Sciarrino for believing in me. Thank you Wes Wu Unruh, without whom I wouldn't sound so professional, have as many completed thoughts or had easy to use multi-media teaching aids.

George W. Bush for demonstrating just how far a C student can go and reminding me that whatever I did, my brand equity is repairable if I believe in the amends that I make and have the help of my friends.

Thank you all for your support.

Benjamin Garth Siddhartha Mack

Index

237